BAKE

BAKE

LORRAINE PASCALE

125 SHOW-STOPPING RECIPES, MADE SIMPLE

bluebird
books for life

CONTENTS

INTRODUCTION

I fell in love with baking at an early age, although I'm not sure if it was baking that I loved at first, or the joy of eating raw dough before it hit the oven! Growing up with the nickname Hollow Legs, I have always loved to eat, and would consume copious amounts of food whenever and wherever possible. My anticipation of visiting friends was based purely on how much there would be to eat – whether it was egg sandwiches followed by shortbread biscuits at Tracey's house, or digestive biscuits and squashed fly biscuits at Tammy's house. Sometimes, it would be chocolate digestive biscuits at home. I would hold up the chocolate biscuits as close as I could to the two-bar electric heater in the corner of the living room, chocolate side facing the orange glowing bars. My trick was to hold it there for as long as possible, until the chocolate started going shiny and sliding down the biscuit, and then to blow on it gently and slowly lick the chocolate off, being sure to catch any on my fingers. Finally, creeping into the kitchen, I would throw the naked biscuit in the bin under rubbish so I wouldn't be found out, reach into the tin for another chocolate-covered beauty, and start all over again!

It was during my first year of school that I realized I could actually bake myself. When I was five years old, my beautiful primary school teacher Mrs Tutton announced that we would have a baking day at school. She gave us a list of the ingredients we'd need to bring along, weighed out in a tin. I remember skipping home as fast as I could and waiting patiently for my mum to wake up from her sleep after working nights. Pacing up and down with excitement, I decided to take the matter into my own hands, and started weighing the ingredients. Soon I was covered in flour, icing sugar, jam and butter, and the kitchen was turned inside out. My mother came thundering down the stairs at the cacophony … needless to say, things did not end well and I was sent upstairs in a floury, blubbering mess after being reprimanded for waking her up and making the kitchen look as if little elves had thrown a baking party!

Despite the false start, the next day I headed to school with a battered old tin full of the ingredients, as happy as Larry. One of the most vivid moments of my childhood is carefully unwrapping each ingredient, putting it into the bowl and listening with much more interest than usual as we creamed, sieved, mixed and dolloped the ingredients into each other, onto the tray and into the oven. I licked the bowl clean and decided at that moment that baking was a very good thing to do.

Bake for pleasure

I recently tweeted about baking and asked what it means to people, and similar messages came back over and over again: we do it on the weekends or in our spare time, when we are feeling low, when we want to relax, when we want to make others happy. And that is what baking is for me. People have theorized that baking must be replacing some kind of missing ingredient from my very challenging past, but I don't see it like that. With so many of us feeling disconnected in this world of stress, social media and quick fixes, baking is something that cannot be rushed. It needs time and gives us a chance to slow down and be in the moment.

Baking has recently enjoyed a renaissance on our TV screens. The secret to its success is that baking is not a fad, or a passing phase. There will forever be a birthday, wedding or even an office party where baking can take centre stage. The TV shows have simply reminded us of the beauty of baking and how it can bring us together, and I just love that idea. I developed #bakeandshare on my social media so that bakers can share their creations with an online community. I like to repost the incredible bakes on my social media channels so we can all 'ooh' and 'aah' at their beauty. I think that this sharing element is so important, both with loved ones and online. We are more connected than ever on social media, but true, authentic connections are becoming fewer by the day. I believe there are few things that can connect people in the way that baking can.

Bake with a twist

I know lots of you have many baking bibles lining your shelves, written by well-known TV chefs, famous writers and bloggers. I do too. Therefore, I wanted to create a book that was unique in its offering, and that would complement the books you already have. There are many classic recipes in the book that are must-haves in any baker's repertoire, but I have given them something a little different to widen your baking horizons and get that 'wow' factor.

These are aspirational and achievable recipes that can take you step by step through the baking process, giving you bakes that are fresh, delicious and stunning. I've updated some old classics such as Battenberg cake, giving you a chocolate and espresso flavour and a striking finish (see Chocolate espresso and almond Battenburg cake, page 142). I've included the old faithful Swiss roll, but have injected a burst of colour and fun (see Out of Africa giraffe Swiss roll with orange cream filling, page 145). There are also brand new, surprisingly simple decoration techniques, such as petal ombre icing (see Lavender ombre cake with petal icing, page 234).

Bake like a pro

People always ask me how to improve at baking. The first thing I always say is to use the best ingredients you can afford – organic really is the best, but it is also very expensive. I would suggest that if you have fresh fruit in your recipe, then it is definitely worth spending extra money on it, but there is no need to spend lots on fancy butter – regular butter works just fine as long as it is butter, not margarine. To keep things simple, all of the recipes in the book use salted butter and medium-sized eggs unless they state otherwise. I'd also say that weighing ingredients accurately is a big, fat baking must.

If you are vegan, you may wish to try egg replacers – there are lots on the market and some work better than others, so it's a case of trial and error to get the right balance. I really love Doves gluten-free flour, as it works so well in many recipes. If you are looking for tasty gluten-free pastry, I would suggest using one of my recipes (see pages 276–7), or as a shortcut I have seen some really good gluten-free ready-made pastries in the supermarket.

It sounds obvious, but it is really important to follow the recipe to the letter – don't freestyle on anything, from tin size and shape to oven temperature, ingredients or technique. There are many different techniques in the book: creaming, mixing, piping, folding pastry and whipping up meringues. Take your time to read the instructions – something that I am not always so good at, being a little impatient at times! If you are trying a completely new technique for the first time, my advice is to take your time over it, and remember that it's okay not to get things right immediately. Always leave more time than you think you'll need, and unless the recipe states otherwise, you can even bake the day before you want to serve. I have avoided giving preparation times as we all work at a different pace – at baking school, they called me the 'galloping gourmet', which would delight the teachers, although I would leave a big old mess in my wake!

For truly show-stopping results, don't forget the presentation. There are so many things that can make your creations stand out. If you want a quick and easy decoration tip, then fresh flowers work wonders! You can also use some simple piping effects on top, or sprinkle over a little grated chocolate.

I love the magic and art of baking, as well as the wonders it can do for morale. Hopefully you will find inspiration in this book to take your baking skills to the next level and beyond. I can't wait to see your creations. #bakeandshare

Lorraine x

EQUIPMENT

I recommend that you do your homework before you buy equipment, even on the cheapest items. There is good advice on the internet – Amazon reviews are really helpful. I recommend places like eBay for second-hand items such as stand mixers, but make sure whatever you buy is returnable. These days there are also great new mixers and processors available in a wide range of price brackets. This list of equipment is not exhaustive, but I wanted to give an idea of the key items I love, to help you become your best baker yet.

Scales Measuring is everything! I recommend a good set of electronic scales. You can find some great ones that only cost a few pounds.

Measuring spoons So many of us reach in to the cutlery draw to pull out any old spoon, but it's really important to invest in some measuring spoons – they usually come in a set with ½ teaspoon, I teaspoon, I tablespoon etc.

Bowls Get a good selection of bowls of different sizes, both in metal and glass. I don't use plastic ones, as I find that flavours linger in the bowl.

Stand mixer I experimented with a cheap mixer, but found I had to buy another one as it was so bad. If you buy cheap you buy twice! This does not mean you have to go for the most expensive mixers, though – have a look for brands that you know well and read the reviews, as there are many good-value options out there. Make sure the attachments are made of a solid material such as metal, because the plastic ones do not mix as well. Some attachments have a little piece of plastic on them that helps to pick up all of the mixture when mixing – make sure this is sturdy.

Hand-held electric whisk This is great if you don't want to use a stand mixer, especially for smaller bakes and for whisking up a few eggs for meringues.

Rolling pin I have recently invested in a metal rolling pin, which I love. It's awesome as it stays cold – great for pastry, as it often needs to keep cool.

Spatula A large plastic spatula is an absolute must – it's great for scooping mixture out of bowls, making sure you reach each and every last bit!

Palette knives I have an assortment of these in different sizes – long ones for frosting cakes and small ones for decorating and levelling out cakes before they are baked.

Bench scraper I use this more than anything else. It's great for picking up bread, or cutting up bread or pastry. It's also good for frosting cakes and even for tidying up flour on the work surface.

Tins Dark-coloured tins cook mixture faster than lighter tins. When you are using a darker tin, the bake may – and I do say may! – need a shorter cooking time, so keep that in mind. Loose-bottomed tins make life so much easier, as you can quickly pop cakes out rather than having a little battle with your bake! Having said that, if you line and grease your tins well, then a cake should always come out cleanly.

Pastry brush You need a pastry brush to glaze certain breads or cakes before or after baking. I like to use brushes with bristles rather than plastic ones, but look out as even good-quality ones can sometimes shed bristles as you use them! Silicone brushes are fine but you do not get such an even glaze.

Piping nozzles Avoid plastic nozzles, as they don't give the clean and sharp lines you can achieve with metal ones.

Cutters Go for metal cookie cutters instead of plastic ones – these will give you cleaner lines and a sharper-looking cookie.

Mechanical ice-cream scoop These are great for portioning mixture and dough out in equal size.

Microplane shaver I love microplane shavers – they help to get really fine citrus zest. If you are colouring your sponge cakes, you can also use a microplane to lightly shave off a top layer of sponge to reveal colour beneath.

Rotating cake stand I have a plastic rotating cake stand that works well, but I also just invested in a metal one that rotates even more smoothly, making it easy to achieve flawless frosted cakes.

Sugar thermometer I much prefer digital probe thermometers to the old-school style, as they are much more accurate and quicker than other thermometers. I use mine all the time.

Oven thermometer Test the temperature of your oven by placing an oven thermometer on the middle shelf. This will show the oven's true temperature compared to what it says on the dial. You may be surprised by what you see – my oven is about 50°C (120°F) out, and thanks to the thermometer, I always get the temperature right for my bakes.

Pizza stone If your oven seems to burn the bottom of your bakes, even when you have checked the temperature, then invest in a pizza stone and place this in the bottom of the oven. This will throw the heat up and around the food to give you an even bake, and is especially helpful for gas ovens.

COOKIES & BISCUITS

CHOCOLATE & VANILLA STARS

I really love baking with other people – sharing the process with a friend or family member can be very therapeutic and fun. These stars look great, and are perfect for making with children. They are also awesome as presents! For a harmonious black and white design, line up all of the centres carefully before they are baked.

Using a wooden spoon, cream together the butter and sugar in a bowl, until the mixture is lighter and fluffier. Add the vanilla and beat in the egg. Divide the mixture into two separate bowls. Add the cocoa powder into one of the bowls and mix until well combined, and then add 150g of the flour to each bowl and briskly stir until well combined.

Using your hands, bring each mixture together into a dough. I sort of squidge the mixture on the side of the bowl to do this. Wrap each dough in cling film and chill for 10–30 minutes to firm up and make the dough easier to handle.

Line two large baking sheets with baking parchment. On a lightly floured surface, roll out the plain cookie dough until it is 5mm thick. Using the 9cm cutter, stamp out twelve large stars, placing each cookie on a lined baking sheet as you go. When you have cut out all of the stars you can, scrunch up the dough and re-roll it to the same thickness, then stamp out more stars. Using the 3cm cutter, stamp out a small star from the centre of each large star, and place these small stars on a sheet of baking parchment and set aside.

Roll out the chocolate dough between two sheets of baking parchment until it is 5mm thick. If it sticks, sprinkle over a little cocoa powder (this helps to keep the colour dark). Using the 9cm cutter, stamp out twelve large stars, putting them on the second lined baking sheet as you go. Stamp out a small star from the centre of each one, and place them on a sheet of baking parchment.

Slot the smaller chocolate stars into the centres of the large vanilla stars. Repeat the process with the large chocolate stars and smaller vanilla stars, and then place the twenty-four black and white cookies in the fridge to firm up for 15 minutes. Preheat the oven to 180°C (fan 160°C/350°F/gas 4).

Bake the stars for 10–12 minutes, until they are cooked through and firm, then remove them from the oven and leave to cool on the baking sheets. Serve.

230g butter, softened

200g caster sugar

seeds of ½ vanilla pod or 1 tsp vanilla extract

1 egg

2 tbsp cocoa powder, plus extra for dusting (sifted if lumpy)

300g self-raising flour, plus extra for dusting

Equipment

9cm star-shaped cookie cutter

3cm star-shaped cookie cutter

BIG SOFT CHEWY OATMEAL RAISIN COOKIES

I love oats! Given half the chance, I will eat them straight from the box. The way I eat my porridge baffles most: I add the tiniest bit of water to the pan, heap in the oats and give it all a stir, cooking the mixture for seconds before serving it up while the oats are still pretty much solid. I put oats in my baking as much as possible, either as a star of the show like this, or as a replacement for some flour in recipes to give them more flavour and texture.

Preheat the oven to 180°C (fan 160°C/350°F/gas 4) and line two baking sheets with baking parchment.

Put the butter and the sugar into a bowl and cream them together until the mixture goes light and fluffy. You can do this with a wooden spoon, but if you have a stand mixer or hand-held electric whisk then it will be much easier and quicker. Add the egg and vanilla and beat well, and then stir in the raisins, flour and oats along with the pinch of salt.

Bring the mixture together, using as few stirs as possible so that the mixture of stretchy proteins (gluten) in the flour does not become overworked and tough. When the mixture is fully combined, divide it into ten equal-sized blobs (each about 50g), and place them onto the lined baking sheets as you go, leaving room between them so they can spread out.

Place the sheets in the oven and bake for 8–10 minutes. The trick is to take them out of the oven before they are super firm – you want them to be just slightly under-baked so that they are still chewy when they cool. Once they are ready, remove them from the oven and leave them to cool for a little while before serving. These are so difficult to resist when they are warm!

100g butter, softened

100g soft light brown sugar

1 egg

seeds of 1 vanilla pod or 2 tsp vanilla extract

70g raisins

50g self-raising flour

130g porridge oats

pinch of salt

Equipment

stand mixer or hand-held electric whisk (optional)

MELTING MOMENTS WITH OATS AND VANILLA

When I was at boarding school, we sometimes used to cook at the weekends, and we loved making these incredibly easy melting moments. The best part was eating the uncooked cookie dough (of course I do not advocate that, but oh my goodness, it is good!). Watch them disappear when they come out of the oven – it's hard to find someone who doesn't like them.

225g butter, softened

120g caster sugar

I egg

seeds of ½ vanilla pod or 2 tsp vanilla extract

180g porridge oats, plus large handful for rolling

275g self-raising flour

Equipment
stand mixer or hand-held electric whisk (optional)

Preheat the oven to 180°C (fan 160°C/350°F/gas 4) and line two baking sheets with baking parchment.

Put the butter and sugar into a bowl and cream them together until the mixture goes light and fluffy. If you have a stand mixer or hand-held electric whisk then it will be much easier and quicker to do this, but a wooden spoon works too – I certainly used a wooden spoon to make these at school!

Add the egg and beat well, and then add the vanilla, oats and flour. Mix until just combined, using as few stirs as possible so that the mixture of stretchy proteins (gluten) in the flour does not become overworked and tough.

Put a large handful of oats on the work surface. Take I heaped tablespoon of the dough (about 50g) and then using your hands, roll the mixture into a ball. Gently roll the ball in the porridge oats and place it on the lined baking sheet, pressing it down lightly. Repeat with the rest of the mixture to give you about eighteen biscuits, spacing them apart as they will spread out a bit in the oven.

Place the biscuits into the oven and bake for 12–14 minutes, or until they are cooked through and have turned a lovely golden brown.

Once the melting moments are baked, remove them from the oven and leave them to cool for a little while before serving.

ALMOND & APRICOT
THUMBPRINT COOKIES

I love that baking is so tactile. I am not very good at art, pottery or sculpture, so I get my creative outlet from cooking. This recipe is a 'must do' with the kiddies – there will be mess and jam will end up in everyone's hair, but it will be a fun session with an incredibly tasty result.

Line two baking sheets with baking parchment. Put the butter and sugar together in a bowl and beat it really well until it becomes lighter and fluffier. I like to use my stand mixer fitted with a paddle attachment for this, but a hand-held electric whisk also works, as does a wooden spoon with a bit of elbow grease.

Add the egg yolk, flour and the ground almonds to the butter and sugar mixture and gently mix together until everything is combined – the dough should be quite stiff. Form the dough into a ball and wrap it in cling film, then squish the ball down a little. Place the dough in the fridge for a good hour to firm up.

Preheat the oven to 180°C (fan 160°C/350°F/gas 4) and remove the dough from the fridge. Pull off a bit of the dough (about 50g) and roll it into a ball, about 5cm across. Place the ball on one of the lined baking sheets. Using your thumb, press the centre of the ball so you almost touch the sheet. Repeat with the rest of the dough, to give you twelve cookies in total. Allow plenty of room between each cookie so it can expand. If the dough becomes a little soft then place it into the fridge for 20 minutes to firm up (or into the freezer for 10 minutes).

Fill each thumbprint with 1 teaspoon of the apricot jam, and bake the cookies for 12–15 minutes, or until they are firm to the touch but not too dark in colour.

Remove the baked cookies from the oven and leave them to cool down before you eat them – be careful as the jam gets super hot. Dust with icing sugar, if you like, and serve.

200g butter, softened

100g caster sugar

1 egg yolk

225g plain flour

50g ground almonds

60g apricot jam

icing sugar, to decorate (optional)

Equipment

stand mixer or hand-held electric whisk (optional)

COFFEE, MAPLE & WALNUT BISCOTTI

Biscotti originated in Italy, where they are traditionally served with coffee. They are a very firm cookie, so they can be dunked into a hot drink without going all soggy. I think they're lovely to serve on a cold day when you are with friends, or at home by yourself enjoying a peaceful moment with a large cup of hot coffee.

Preheat the oven to 180°C (fan 160°C/350°F/gas 4) and line a large baking sheet with baking parchment. Mix together the flour, baking powder, bicarbonate of soda, sugar, maple syrup, walnuts, raisins and salt in a large bowl.

Make a well in the centre of the mixture and stir in the eggs, vanilla and coffee essence until the mixture starts to come together and form clumps, then put down the spoon and bring the dough together in a ball with your hands. With lightly floured hands, roll the dough into a long sausage shape, about 30cm long and 5cm wide. Lift the shaped dough onto the lined baking sheet and press it down gently until it is about 1.5cm high.

Bake the biscotti dough in the oven for 25–30 minutes, until it has risen and spread. It should feel nice and firm but still look relatively pale in colour. Remove it from the oven and leave for a few minutes, until cool enough to handle, then turn the oven down to 140°C (fan 120°C/275°F/gas 1).

Using a bread knife, cut the biscotti sausage diagonally into 1cm-thick slices. Biscotti are quite crumbly so it is best to use a sharp serrated knife.

Line the baking sheet with fresh baking parchment and arrange the biscotti on top. Bake them for another 15 minutes, then turn them over and bake again for another 10–15 minutes, until they are nice and firm and look dry.

Remove the baked biscotti from the oven and leave to cool completely. You could pack them into boxes or cellophane bags tied with a pretty ribbon to make great gifts, or store in an airtight tin for up to a month. Serve with a nice warm drink.

200g wholemeal or plain flour, plus a little extra

1 tsp baking powder

1 tsp bicarbonate of soda

60g soft light brown sugar

20g maple syrup

80g walnuts, chopped

60g raisins

pinch of salt

2 eggs, beaten

seeds of ½ vanilla pod or 1 tsp vanilla extract

1 tsp Camp coffee essence

CRANBERRY, STAR ANISE & CHOCOLATE FLORENTINES

I'm not a big fan of regular Florentines – there's something about the combination of mixed peel and glacé cherries that's not my thing – so I have made these versions a little different while still true to their basic structure and chewy, crunchy and chocolatey form. Ground star anise loses its flavour quickly, so I recommend that you buy fresh star anise and grind it using a spice grinder or pestle and mortar.

60g soft light brown sugar

60g butter

½ tsp ground star anise

pinch of ground nutmeg

1 tbsp maple syrup

pinch of salt

60g plain white flour (or substitute with Doves Farm gluten-free plain flour)

80g dried cranberries, finely chopped

50g blanched almonds, finely chopped

70g milk chocolate, roughly chopped

Preheat the oven to 180°C (fan 160°C/350°F/gas 4) and line two large baking sheets with baking parchment.

Put the sugar, butter and star anise in a pan along with the nutmeg, maple syrup and salt. Place the pan over a low heat and heat through until the butter melts, stirring with a wooden spoon, and then remove the pan from the heat and add the flour, cranberries and almonds. Mix this all together with the wooden spoon.

Take 1 heaped teaspoon of the mixture and put it onto one of the lined baking sheets. Repeat with the rest of the mixture, spacing each spoon well apart as they will spread in the oven. Place the Florentines in the oven and bake for 8–10 minutes, until they have spread a little and are golden brown. Once they are baked, remove them from the oven and leave them to cool completely on the baking sheets.

Once the Florentines have cooled, melt the chocolate in a heatproof bowl set over a pan of simmering water. Make sure that the base of the bowl does not touch the water as this may cause the chocolate to clump into a grainy lump. You can also melt the chocolate in the microwave in 40-second blasts, stirring well between each blast.

Using a palette knife, flip the Florentines over and drizzle the melted chocolate over the flat side of each one. Once you have drizzled all of the Florentines, leave them to set for a couple of minutes and then they are ready to serve.

Most bakeries spread the underside of Florentines with a layer of chocolate and then mark them with a fork, but I like to simply drizzle with chocolate – it is easy, quick and much more fun!

MINT CHOCOLATE PINWHEELS

I try to avoid using artificial flavourings in my baking, however mint flavouring is an exception, because it's hard to extract flavour from fresh mint leaves. You can leave out the mint flavouring and colour if you wish, to make chocolate and vanilla pinwheels. Rolling the dough between sheets of baking parchment means you don't have to use lots of flour, which can mute the wonderful colours of the finished pinwheels. **PICTURED ON PAGES 26–7.**

Cream together the butter and sugar in a large bowl with a wooden spoon or hand-held electric whisk. Add the vanilla and salt and then beat in the egg.

Divide the mixture between two separate bowls. Beat the cocoa powder and coffee into one bowl and the mint extract and a few drops of food colouring into the other bowl. Add 150g of the flour to each bowl and briskly stir until well combined. Using your hands, squidge the chocolate mixture together to form a ball, then wrap it in cling film and place in the fridge for 30 minutes to firm up. Repeat with the mint dough.

Once the doughs are firm, roll the chocolate dough between two pieces of baking parchment to a rectangle, 30 x 25cm in size. Repeat this process with the mint dough, and place both rectangles in the fridge for at least 10 minutes.

When the rolled-out doughs are firm, remove them from the fridge and peel the top piece of baking parchment from each one. Flip the mint dough and place it on top of the chocolate dough, lining up the corners. Peel off the top piece of baking parchment, and then with one of the shorter edges facing you, use the parchment to roll the dough into a tight sausage shape. It is important to get the very first bit rolled in tightly so you see the lovely swirl.

Wrap the rolled dough in cling film and chill for a further 30 minutes to ensure the dough is very firm. Preheat the oven to 180°C (fan 160°C/350°F/gas 4) and line two large baking sheets with baking parchment. Remove the cling film from the dough roll. Using a very sharp knife, cut the cookies into twenty-four slices, each 1cm thick. Put each slice straight onto the baking sheets as you go, allowing them plenty of room to spread out.

Bake the biscuits for 15–20 minutes, or until they are cooked through. These biscuits remain a little soft when they are baked, but they will firm up as they cool. Once baked, leave them to cool completely before serving.

220g butter, softened

225g caster sugar

seeds of 1 vanilla pod or 2 tsp vanilla extract

pinch of salt

1 egg

3 tbsp cocoa powder

2 tsp instant coffee powder mixed with 2 tsp boiling water

2 tsp mint extract

few drops of green food colouring

300g self-raising flour

Equipment
hand-held electric whisk (optional)

MELTING VIENNESE WHIRLS

I have an addiction to these: I absolutely must have more than one! My love affair started when I was pregnant – I would go for the weekly shop at the supermarket and head straight for the biscuit aisle. Tearing open a box, I would proceed to eat the whole darn thing as I wandered around throwing food into my trolley. Buttery, crumbly and sweet, these homemade versions are simply perfect! **PICTURED ON PAGES 26–7.**

225g butter, softened

50g icing sugar, plus extra for dusting

seeds of 1 vanilla pod or 2 tsp vanilla extract

1 egg

30g cornflour

225g plain flour

pinch of salt

3 tbsp whole milk

For the filling

50g butter, softened

100g icing sugar

seeds of ½ vanilla pod or 1 tsp vanilla extract

For the jam

60g seedless raspberry jam

Equipment

piping bag with 1.5cm star nozzle

piping bag with 2cm star nozzle (optional)

Preheat the oven to 180°C (fan 160°C/350°F/gas 4) and line two baking sheets with baking parchment.

Cream together the butter, icing sugar and vanilla using a wooden spoon until the mixture is a little lighter and fluffier. Add the egg and mix to combine, and then add the cornflour, flour, salt and milk. Use a spatula to fold it all together until the dough is smooth and uniform.

Spoon the mixture into the piping bag fitted with the 1.5cm star nozzle and then pipe 4cm rosettes onto the lined baking sheets. Repeat until you have used up all of the mixture – you should get twenty-eight biscuits.

Pop the biscuits into the oven and bake for 10–12 minutes, or until the biscuits are pale golden brown and firm. When they are baked, remove them from the oven and leave to cool completely.

As the biscuits are cooling, make the filling. Mix together the butter and icing sugar in a bowl with the vanilla. Beat really hard until the mixture is light and fluffy. I usually do this with a wooden spoon as the amount of mixture is too small for a stand mixer or hand-held electric whisk.

When the biscuits are completely cool, turn fourteen of them over so that they are flat-side up, and spoon a small blob of the buttercream filling onto their flat side. You could also pipe on the buttercream using a piping bag fitted with a 2cm star-shaped nozzle, if you fancy.

Give the jam a good stir to loosen it up a little and then top the buttercream with 1 teaspoon of jam. Place the remaining biscuits on top to sandwich the filling, so you end up with fourteen delicious biscuits.

Put the Viennese whirls on a plate, dust with some icing sugar and serve.

RASPBERRY JAMMIE DODGERS

These are part of the British biscuit brigade, but I make no apologies when I say that you can't beat a homemade version! I have suggested using a heart-shaped cutter instead of the usual round to make them a bit different. It is also fun to make miniature varieties and serve them on sticks for a party. I like to use seedless raspberry jam for these, but you can also use strawberry, cherry or even lemon curd as a filling. **PICTURED ON PAGES 26–7.**

Cream together the sugar and butter in a bowl. Add the vanilla and beat in the egg, and then gradually stir in the flour and almonds until it is all combined. Squidge the dough together, wrap it in cling film and put it in the fridge for at least 10 minutes or up to 30 minutes, until firm.

Preheat the oven to 180°C (fan 160°C/350°F/gas 4) and line two large baking sheets with baking parchment. Roll out the dough on a lightly floured surface to 5mm thickness and cut out twenty-four rounds with the 8cm cutter. Arrange them on the lined baking sheets. Using the 3cm cutter, stamp out a smaller heart or round from the centre of twelve of the biscuit rounds. Remove the small hearts or rounds, wrap them in cling film and then put them in the fridge in an airtight container to bake on another day.

Bake all of the large biscuits for 10–12 minutes, until cooked through, and then remove them from the oven and leave them to cool. These biscuits remain pale and a little soft when baked, but they will firm up as they cool.

Put the jam in a bowl and stir in the lemon juice or water to loosen up. Once the biscuits are completely cool, they are ready for the jam. Dollop 1 heaped teaspoon of jam into the centre of one of the whole round biscuits, leaving a border of about 1.5cm all the way round the outside of the biscuit. This will make sure that the jam does not squelch out of the sides when the top goes on. Repeat with the rest of the whole biscuit rounds.

Place one of the biscuits with the cut-out centre on top of a jam-topped biscuit. Press it down gently and then repeat with the other biscuits. Sprinkle over some icing sugar to serve. These are best eaten on the day they are made. If you are making them in advance, keep the biscuits in an airtight container and fill them with jam just before serving.

100g caster sugar

200g butter, softened

seeds of ½ vanilla pod or 1 tsp vanilla extract

1 egg

280g plain flour, plus extra for dusting

60g ground almonds

icing sugar, for dusting

For the filling

100g jam (I love raspberry seedless)

1 tsp lemon juice or water

Equipment

8cm straight-sided round cookie cutter

3cm straight-sided heart-shaped or round cookie cutter

COCONUT & STEM GINGER MACAROONS

Unlike French macarons, which many people find a challenge, these old-school coconut versions are nice and easy to make, but taste equally good. Versatile coconut seems to be in everything at the moment – the ingredient isn't always to my taste, but as the integral part of a macaroon, coconut is simply delicious.

5 egg whites

2 tbsp caster sugar

I tbsp honey

I tbsp stem ginger, very finely chopped

150g desiccated coconut

2 tbsp plain flour

Equipment

non-stick silicone baking mat (optional)

Preheat the oven to 160°C (fan 140°C/325°F/gas 3) and if you are using a baking sheet rather than a silpat mat, line it with baking parchment.

Place the egg whites in a bowl and whisk until frothy, then add the sugar, honey, stem ginger, coconut and flour and mix it all together until you have a sticky, quite wet mixture.

Divide the mixture into fourteen equal-sized pieces (roughly 27g each). I find the best way to do this is by making my hands a little bit wet, then rolling each piece into a ball and squidging it into a pyramid shape. Make sure to really squeeze the mixture together tightly so that it doesn't fall apart.

When you have formed each macaroon, place it onto the lined baking sheet or silicone baking mat. Bake the macaroons for about 20 minutes, or until they are going a light golden brown but are still nice and soft inside.

Once the macaroons are baked, remove them from the oven and set aside to cool before serving.

LEBKUCHEN-STYLE COOKIES

These spiced cookies are protected in status – they can only be called Lebkuchen if they have been made in the city of Nuremberg in Germany. The dough has a tacky, malleable texture that is easy to cut out, and it doesn't spread too much during baking, making the shapes attractively sharp. This dough gets better with age so, if possible, make the dough and leave it in the fridge for up to 2 days before you need to use it.

Put the butter, soft light brown sugar, honey, cinnamon, ginger, nutmeg, vanilla and salt into a pan and heat gently until the butter has melted and the sugar has dissolved. Turn up the heat a little and allow it to boil for a couple of minutes, then remove it from the heat and pour it into a large bowl. Let the mixture cool down a little.

Once the mixture has cooled, add the flour and the bicarbonate of soda and mix everything together to combine. Get your hands in the bowl and form it into a large ball, then wrap it in cling film and pop it into the fridge to firm up for at least 1 hour and up to 2 days to allow the gluten to relax, making it easier for you to roll out. The dough becomes very firm, so when you wish to use it you will need to leave it out of the fridge for about 30 minutes before rolling.

When you are ready to bake the cookies, preheat the oven to 180°C (fan 160°C/350°F/gas 4) and line two baking sheets with baking parchment. Cut the cookie dough into quarters and roll one piece out on a lightly floured surface to the thickness of a £1 coin (about 3mm).

Using the star cutter, stamp out about eight stars, placing the cookies on one of the lined baking sheets as you go. Re-roll the remaining dough trimmings and continue to make the cookies in this way until all the dough is used up – you should end up with about forty in total. Bake the cookies in batches in the oven for 8–10 minutes. or until the cookies are just going a little darker golden brown and are firmer to the touch.

While the cookies are baking, make the lemon glaze. Mix the glaze ingredients in a bowl and set aside until needed. Once the cookies are baked, remove them from the oven and brush with the lemon glaze, then leave the cookies to cool down completely on wire racks. The cookies make a lovely gift or you could just keep them for your friends and family to enjoy.

200g butter

180g soft light brown sugar

100g honey

2 tbsp ground cinnamon

3 tbsp ground ginger

2 tsp ground nutmeg

seeds of 1½ vanilla pods or 3 tsp vanilla extract

pinch of salt

375g plain flour, plus extra for dusting

1 tsp bicarbonate of soda

For the lemon glaze

1 tbsp lemon juice

1 tbsp water

60g icing sugar (sifted if lumpy)

Equipment

9cm star-shaped cookie cutter

STRAWBERRY, CREME CHANTILLY & AMARETTO SHORTCAKES

These are a new take on the quintessential American strawberry shortcakes, which are scone-like biscuits sandwiched with cream and fresh strawberries. If grown-ups want to be grown up then a splash of Amaretto is just the ticket, but of course you can leave it out if you prefer. Adding some poached rhubarb goes wonderfully with the strawberries, too.

250g plain flour, plus extra for dusting

2 tsp baking powder

65g butter, cold and cut into cubes

65g soft light brown sugar

seeds of ½ vanilla pod or I tsp vanilla extract

165g crème fraiche

I tbsp water

For the fruit filling

225g strawberries, hulled

I tbsp granulated sugar

splash of Amaretto liqueur

For the crème Chantilly

200ml double or whipping cream, cold

seeds of ½ vanilla pod or I tsp vanilla extract

40g icing sugar, plus extra for dusting

Equipment

food processor (optional)

7cm fluted round cookie cutter

Preheat the oven to 200°C (fan 180°C/400°F/gas 6) and lightly dust a large baking sheet with flour.

Place the flour, baking powder, butter and soft light brown sugar in a bowl and rub everything together until it resembles fine breadcrumbs. You can also use a food processor for this. Add the vanilla and crème fraiche with the water and mix together with a round-bladed knife until it starts to clump together into a soft dough, then bring it all together with your hands into a ball. Tip the ball out onto a lightly floured work surface and squish it down with your hands or a rolling pin until it is about 2cm thick. Using the cookie cutter, stamp out twelve rounds and place them on the prepared baking sheet as you go.

Place the rounds in the oven and bake for 10–15 minutes, until cooked through and golden brown. Once they are baked, remove them from the oven and leave to cool on the baking sheet.

Meanwhile, make the fruit filling. Cut the strawberries into slices and place them in a bowl with the granulated sugar and Amaretto. Stir to combine and then leave to sit at room temperature to allow the flavours to develop while the shortcakes are baking.

Once the shortcakes have cooled down, make the crème Chantilly. Put the cream, vanilla and icing sugar in a bowl and whisk until the mixture thickens and reaches soft peaks. You want it to be shiny but not super stiff. If you over-whisk it, add ½ tablespoon of milk to thin it out a little.

Put a shortcake onto each plate and spread over half of the crème Chantilly. Arrange the sliced strawberries on top, draining off and discarding excess liquid, then cover with the rest of the crème Chantilly and place a shortcake on top of each one. Add a light dusting of icing sugar to serve.

CHOCOLATE & SALTED CARAMEL ICE-CREAM SANDWICHES

Before you start this recipe, check that you have enough freezer space and set aside 1–3 hours to allow the ice-cream tubs to melt in your sink or a large bowl. This method gives very neat results, but if it sounds like too much trouble, then you can simply sandwich the cookies together with a scoop of ice cream. If you wish to keep the ice-cream sandwiches for more than a day, wrap each one individually with cling film to prevent freezer burn.

Line the cake tins or large roasting tin with a double layer of cling film. Pour 1.5 tubs of the melted ice cream into each cake tin. If you are using a large roasting tin then pour all of the ice cream into that. Put your tin(s) into the freezer until the ice cream has frozen solid.

Choose a baking sheet that can fit into your freezer. Line it with baking parchment. When the ice cream has frozen solid, use the cookie cutter to stamp out eight rounds, placing them on the lined baking sheet as you go. Work quickly – if the ice cream starts to melt, then pop it back into the freezer to firm up. When all the rounds are cut out, put them back into the freezer and continue with the recipe. Keep any leftover ice cream for another day.

To make the cookies, cream together the butter and sugar in a bowl using a wooden spoon until light and fluffy, then beat in the egg. Mix in the flour and cocoa powder, stir well to combine and then get your hands in the bowl to bring it all together. Wrap the dough in cling film and put it in the fridge for about 10 minutes to firm up.

Line two large baking sheets with baking parchment and dust the work surface with cocoa powder. Roll out the cookie dough until it is about 5mm thick, and stamp out sixteen rounds using the cutter, placing them on the baking sheets as you go. Place the rounds into the fridge for 10 minutes to firm up.

Preheat the oven to 180°C (fan 160°C/350°F/gas 4) and bake the rounds for 10–12 minutes, until just firm. Remove the cookies from the oven and use the cutter to trim the edges from each one, then leave to cool down completely.

Once the cookies have cooled, remove the ice-cream rounds from the freezer and sandwich each one with two cookies. Stack them in the tin(s) and put them in the freezer. Remove the ice-cream sandwiches from the freezer 10 minutes or so before you want to serve them, so that they are easy to eat.

3 x 750ml tubs of salted caramel ice cream (I use Häagen Daz), melted

225g butter, softened

200g soft light brown sugar

I egg

140g plain flour

50g cocoa powder, plus extra for dusting (sifted if lumpy)

Equipment

2 x 20cm square cake tins, or I large and very clean roasting tin

9cm straight-sided round cookie cutter

THYME & PARMESAN OATCAKES

Homemade oatcakes are a revelation. The crumbly dough may seem a bit of a struggle, but they are completely worth the effort. Fresh from the oven, the background flavour of the Parmesan and thyme tastes great without a topping, but they are particularly delicious with a sharp Cheddar, some creamy Brie or a fragrant blue cheese. I also eat them with soup or even hummus.

Preheat the oven to 180°C (fan 160°C/350°F/gas 4) and line two baking sheets with baking parchment.

Toss the oats, flour, thyme, Parmesan, bicarbonate of soda and salt together in a large bowl. Add the butter and then pick up bits of the mixture with the tips of your fingers, rubbing it between your fingers and your thumb until all of the butter has been 'rubbed in' and you have a uniform crumb mixture.

Gradually add the cold water, continuing to stir the mixture with a small round-bladed knife until you get a thick and quite solid dough. Tip the dough out onto a work surface lightly dusted with flour and knead it into a ball.

Roll the dough out until it is just under the thickness of a £1 coin (about 3mm). Stamp out the oatcakes with the cookie cutter, placing them onto the lined baking sheets as you go – you should get about thirty in total. The oatcake mixture is quite crumbly, but just keep squishing it back together with your hands if it starts to break up.

Bake the oatcakes in the oven for 20 minutes, then turn them over and bake them for another 5–10 minutes, or until the oatcakes are golden brown and firm to the touch. They should be crisp and dried out – you can check by trying to snap one in half.

Once the oatcakes are cooked, remove them from the oven and leave to cool completely on a wire rack. They are totally delicious with your favourite cheese and chutney, and will keep in an airtight container for a couple of weeks.

200g rolled oats

75g wholemeal flour, plus a little extra for dusting

1 tbsp fresh thyme leaves, finely chopped

40g Parmesan cheese, freshly grated

large pinch of bicarbonate of soda

pinch of salt

25g butter, cold and cut into cubes

125ml cold water

Equipment

6cm straight-sided round cookie cutter

BROWNIES & TRAYBAKES

GOLDEN SYRUP & BROWN SUGAR GINGER FLAPJACKS

I have written many recipes for flapjacks in my time! Every time I create a new one, I try to make it that little bit better. I love to add a little lemon zest and spice to freshen and liven up the flavour, but if you prefer regular flapjacks then you can just leave these out – the recipe will taste just as good. If you don't have both soft light brown sugar and dark brown sugar then you could just use one of them, making sure the total amount comes to 175g.

Preheat the oven to 180°C (fan 160°C/350°F/gas 4) and line the baking tin with baking parchment. I make sure there is extra baking parchment hanging over the edges – this makes it easier to pull out the flapjacks once they are baked.

Put the butter into a medium pan and add the golden syrup, both kinds of sugar and treacle, if using. Cook gently over a low heat until the sugar has dissolved and the butter has melted, then remove the pan from the heat and add the vanilla, salt, oats, lemon zest, ginger and cinnamon. Mix it all together and then spoon the mixture into the lined tin. Squish it down really well using the back of a wooden spoon.

Use a sharp knife to mark nine or sixteen squares on top of the mixture and then place the tin in the oven for 20–25 minutes, or until the flapjacks are golden brown.

Once the flapjacks are cooked, remove the tin from the oven and leave them to cool for a little bit in the tin. When they are cool, remove them from the tin using the overhanging parchment, cut out the nine or sixteen squares and serve.

180g butter

180g golden syrup

100g soft light brown sugar

75g dark brown sugar

1 tbsp treacle (optional)

seeds of 1 vanilla pod or 2 tsp vanilla extract

pinch of salt

375g porridge oats

zest of ½ lemon

2 tsp ground ginger

pinch of ground cinnamon

Equipment
20cm square cake tin

I like to spend a few minutes squishing down the flapjack mixture in the tin so that it is packed down well – this makes it less likely that the baked flapjacks will crumble when they are cut into squares.

CHIA SEED COCONUT FLAPJACKS WITH LINSEED

Thanks to social media and cooks such as Ella Mills, Tess Ward, Hemsley + Hemsley et al, loads of healthy ingredients are now readily available in the shops. Some ingredients, such as chia seeds, are great for baking – they contain antioxidants, protein, a good amount of fibre and omega 3. These flapjacks are easy to make and nutritious, but be warned that they do contain a fair amount of sugar!

Preheat the oven to 180°C (fan 160°C/350°F/gas 4) and line the baking tin with baking parchment. I make sure there is extra baking parchment hanging over the edges – this makes it easier to pull out the flapjacks once they are baked.

Melt the coconut oil in a small pan or in the microwave and leave to cool a little. Put the rest of the ingredients together in a bowl and mix to combine, and then mix in the melted coconut oil.

Tip the mixture into the lined tin and squish down with a wooden spoon. Spend a good few minutes squishing it down hard, using all of your body weight – spending a little bit of time doing this will stop the flapjacks from falling apart when you cut them.

Use a sharp knife to mark sixteen equal-sized squares on top of the mixture and then place the tin in the oven for 20–25 minutes, or until the flapjacks are firm and just beginning to turn golden brown around the edges.

Once the flapjacks are cooked, remove the tin from the oven and leave them to cool for a little bit in the tin. When they are cool, remove them from the tin using the overhanging parchment, cut out the sixteen squares and serve.

150g extra-virgin coconut oil

180g porridge oats

30g milled chia seed

40g milled linseed

4 tbsp golden syrup

75g soft light brown sugar

Equipment

20cm square cake tin

PEANUT BUTTER PROTEIN FLAPJACKS

This is a cheeky recipe because it doesn't actually require baking! If you want to include more protein in your diet then this recipe is a great way to do so. It can be tricky to choose from the many different protein powders on the market today, but I recommend choosing a powder that is at least 80 per cent protein and isn't full of unrecognizable additives or sugar. I like using vegan protein, as it's often the most additive- and sugar-free option.

300g porridge oats

80g vegan or whey vanilla protein powder (I use Quest)

120g crunchy peanut butter

3 tbsp honey

5 tbsp melted butter or extra-virgin coconut oil

30–150ml water (depending on your choice of protein powder – vegan powder usually requires more water)

Equipment
20cm square cake tin

Line the baking tin with baking parchment. I make sure there is extra baking parchment hanging over the edges – this makes it easy to pull out the flapjacks when they are ready to eat.

Put the porridge oats, protein powder, peanut butter, honey, melted butter or coconut oil and 2 tablespoons of the water into a large bowl and mix together with a wooden spoon. It will be super crumbly, so get your hands in and squeeze it together. If it is really dry then keep adding 2 tablespoons of water as you go, squeezing it well between each addition – you are looking for a mixture that is still crumbly but that comes together.

Tip the mixture into the lined tin and squish it down really, really well so that it does not crumble too much when you cut into it. I put my whole body weight on it to squish it down!

Using a sharp knife, mark the flapjacks into sixteen equal-sized squares and then place them in the fridge to set for at least 2 hours, or overnight if possible.

Once the flapjacks have set, remove them from the fridge. Take them out of the tin with the help of the overhanging baking parchment, then cut out the sixteen squares and serve.

LAMINGTONS

Although I lived in Australia for many years, I never ate a lamington on Australian soil. It wasn't until I was back in the UK that I was offered one for the first time. These Oz treats are tasty squares of sponge covered in chocolate icing and coated in coconut. Recently, evidence has come to light that lamingtons originated in New Zealand, but in many foodie circles the jury is still out on that one! They are fun to make and even more fun to eat.

Preheat the oven to 180°C (fan 160°C/350°F/gas 4) and line the baking tin with baking parchment. I make sure there is extra baking parchment hanging over the edges – this makes it easier to pull out the lamingtons once they are baked.

Cream together the butter and the soft light brown sugar in a large bowl until it is light and fluffy. The easiest way to do this is in a stand mixer or with a hand-held electric whisk, but a wooden spoon will also work.

When the mixture is light and fluffy, add one of the eggs and half of the flour and beat well to combine, then add the remaining eggs and flour and beat well again until the mixture is just uniform. Transfer the mixture into the lined tin and level off with the back of a spoon. Place the tin in the oven and bake for 25–30 minutes, or until a skewer inserted into the centre comes out clean and the cake edges have shrunk away from the inside of the tin. Remove the cake from the oven and then leave to cool completely in the tin.

Once the cake has cooled, pop it into the fridge. Meanwhile, make the icing. Melt the chocolate, butter and milk in a heatproof bowl set over a pan of simmering water, making sure the base of the bowl does not touch the water. Remove the bowl from the heat and stir until smooth, then whisk in the icing sugar and cocoa powder, then the boiling water.

Tip the coconut into a shallow bowl. Take the cake out of the fridge and using the overhanging baking parchment, remove it from the tin. Peel off the baking parchment and then cut the cake into sixteen equal-sized squares.

Using your hands, dip a sponge square into the chocolate icing, gently rolling it all the way round to make sure each side is nicely coated. Wipe off any excess on the side of the bowl and then dip it into the coconut and toss gently to coat each side. Transfer to a wire rack and repeat with the other cakes, then set aside for 15 minutes, or until the icing firms up a bit. Serve.

165g butter, softened

150g soft light brown sugar

3 eggs

160g self-raising flour

300g desiccated coconut

For the chocolate icing

135g dark chocolate, roughly chopped

20g butter

90ml whole milk

110g icing sugar (sifted if lumpy)

1 tbsp cocoa powder (sifted if lumpy)

1 tbsp boiling water

Equipment

20cm square cake tin

stand mixer or hand-held electric whisk (optional)

RED VELVET CREAM CHEESE BROWNIES

I based this recipe on my Oreo brownie recipe. I know there is often the temptation to use low-fat or lower-fat cream cheese, but they are too watery for this bake. As a result, I've suggested opting for a mix of full-fat and low-fat varieties in this recipe, although of course omit the low-fat and go for 220g full-fat if you prefer! You could make these brownies into something special for Valentine's Day by using a heart-shaped cutter if you fancy it.

Preheat the oven to 180°C (fan 160°C/350°F/gas 4) and line the tin with baking parchment. I make sure there is extra baking parchment hanging over the edges – this makes it easier to pull out the brownies when they are baked.

Melt the white chocolate in a heatproof bowl set over a pan of simmering water. Make sure that the base of the bowl does not touch the water. You can also melt the chocolate in the microwave in 30-second bursts, stirring well between each burst. Leave the melted chocolate to cool a little.

Melt the butter in a small pan over a gentle heat and then pour it into a large bowl. Leave it to cool down for a moment and then add the sugar, vanilla and cocoa powder and mix together with a wooden spoon.

Add the eggs and food colouring (I do use rather a lot!) and beat again until evenly combined. Then using a spatula, fold in the white chocolate and stir to combine. Mix in the flour and salt and then tip the combined mixture into the lined baking tin, reserving about 2 tablespoons of the mixture behind in the bowl. Spread the mixture evenly in the tin and then set this aside.

To make the white swirl, put all of the ingredients into a clean bowl and beat together for a few seconds with a wooden spoon until combined. Space out nine dollops of the mixture on top of the brownie mixture in the tin.

Place the reserved 2 tablespoons of red velvet brownie mixture on top and swirl the brownie mixture around in the tin with a knife. If you want the marbling to run throughout the brownie, swirl the mixture deeply into the tin, but don't over-swirl it or the mixture may turn pink! Place the tin onto a baking sheet (to make it easier to move in and out of the oven) and bake it for 25–30 minutes, or until the brownies are springy to the touch but still nice and gooey in the middle. Leave the brownies to cool a little in the tin, then remove it from the tin, cut it up into nine equal-sized squares and enjoy.

80g white chocolate, roughly chopped

100g butter

180g caster sugar

seeds of ½ vanilla pod or 1 tsp vanilla extract

2 tbsp cocoa powder

2 eggs

½ tsp red food colouring (I use Sugarflair)

130g spelt white flour or plain white flour

pinch of salt

For the white swirl

80g full-fat cream cheese (I use Philadelphia)

140g low-fat cream cheese (not the really low-fat one)

2 tbsp spelt white flour or plain white flour

2 tbsp caster sugar

seeds of ½ vanilla pod or 1 tsp vanilla extract

1 egg yolk

Equipment

18cm square cake tin

CHOCOLATE CHIP BROWNIES

As many of you will know, I love to make videos on YouTube. One of them was me visiting bakeries to sample cupcakes in LA. I stumbled on the most divine brownies in Sweet E's Bakery on 3rd Street that were just covered in chocolate chips – they could not look more decadent! This little recipe is therefore inspired by my wonderful find on that day. The added bonus of these brownies is that they are also gluten-free. **PICTURED ON PAGE 45.**

Preheat the oven to 180°C (fan 160°C/350°F/gas 4) and line the baking tin with baking parchment. I make sure there is extra baking parchment hanging over the edges – this makes it easier to pull out the brownies when they are baked.

Melt the butter in a small pan over a low heat, and then take the pan off the heat and add the dark chocolate. Leave the chocolate to melt.

Put the eggs in a bowl and whisk them up until they become a little frothy with a hand-held electric whisk, then gradually add the sugar as if you were making a meringue. To do this, add a quarter of the sugar and then whisk up the egg mixture until it becomes frothy. Then add another quarter, and repeat, whisking it well between each addition, until you have used up all of the sugar. The mixture should be really light, fluffy and foam-like. You can of course do this in your stand mixer using the whisk attachment if you like.

Gently tip the chocolate and butter mixture into the fluffy eggs and sugar. I like to tip it around the sides of the bowl – if you pour it directly into the centre this can knock out all of the air you have whisked in. Gently fold this together, keeping as much air in it as possible. Sieve together the flour and cocoa powder, then add to the bowl from a low height so that it does not knock the air out. Fold this all together using as few stirs as possible.

Very gently tip the mixture into your lined tin and then pop it into the oven for about 25 minutes. When the brownies are cooked, they should be dry on top, but still slightly gooey and fudgy inside – don't be tempted to leave the tin in the oven any longer than this or you may end up with a sponge cake!

When the brownies are cooked, remove the tin from the oven and leave to cool for 5 minutes, and then completely cover the top of the brownies with the chocolate chips. Allow to cool completely, then cut into nine equal-sized squares to serve.

160g butter

160g dark chocolate, roughly chopped

3 eggs

250g soft light brown sugar

85g gluten-free plain flour (or use regular plain flour if you wish)

2 tbsp cocoa powder

200g dark chocolate chips

Equipment

20cm square cake tin

hand-held electric whisk or stand mixer

DO GENTLEMAN PREFER WHITE CHOCOLATE BLONDIES?

An American import, white chocolate blondies are growing in popularity all the time. I have left these plain and simple (but still full of flavour) so if you fancy it, go ahead and dress them up with ingredients such as white chocolate chips or nuts. **PICTURED ON PAGE 45.**

150g butter

150g white chocolate, roughly chopped

3 eggs

2 egg yolks

150g soft light brown sugar

seeds of ½ vanilla pod or ½ tsp vanilla extract

4 tbsp white spelt flour

pinch of salt

75g (3oz) pecan nuts, chopped

Equipment

20cm square cake tin

hand-held electric whisk or stand mixer

Preheat the oven to 190°C (fan 170°C/375°F/gas 5) and line the baking tin with baking parchment. I make sure there is extra baking parchment hanging over the edges – this makes it easier to pull out the blondies when they are baked.

Melt the butter in a small pan over a low heat, and then take the pan off the heat and add the white chocolate. Leave the chocolate to melt.

Put the eggs, egg yolks, sugar and vanilla in a bowl and whisk up with a hand-held electric whisk until it is nice and frothy. Add the flour and gently whisk this all together along with the pinch of salt. You can of course do this in your stand mixer using the whisk attachment if you like.

Pour in the white chocolate and butter mixture along with the pecan nuts and gently fold it all together until well combined.

Pour the mixture into the lined tin and pop it into the oven for about 22–25 minutes. When the blondies are cooked, they should be dry on top, but still slightly gooey and fudgy inside – don't be tempted to leave the tin in the oven any longer than this or you may end up with a sponge cake!

When the blondies are baked, remove them from the oven and leave to cool down a little before cutting into nine equal-sized squares. They will crack as you cut them but that is perfectly normal. The blondies are delicious warm with ice cream or fresh cream, and also great when they have cooled.

RICH ESPRESSO & WALNUT TRAYBAKE

SERVES 8

I don't often drink coffee, having turned to matcha green tea for my daily buzz. However, one of the ways that I do readily enjoy our caffeine friend is in the form of a cake. The flavours bring back memories of my childhood – of being at a friend's house, chatting to the parents and all the while eyeing up the cake sitting on the table next to the Bovril sandwiches and jar of sandwich spread!

Preheat the oven to 180°C (fan 160°C/350°F/gas 4) and line the baking tin with baking parchment. I make sure there is extra baking parchment hanging over the edges – this makes it easier to pull out the cake when it is baked.

Put the butter and crème fraiche into a bowl and add the sugar, then cream this together until light and fluffy. The easiest way to do this is in a stand mixer or with a hand-held electric whisk, but a wooden spoon will also work.

When the mixture is fluffy, add two of the eggs, half of the flour and the baking powder and mix together. Then add the other egg with the rest of the flour along with the coffee essence or cooled coffee. Beat the mixture until just combined and then use a spatula to fold in the walnuts.

Tip the cake mixture into the lined tin and smooth the top down with the back of the spoon. Bake for 30–35 minutes, or until a skewer inserted into the centre of the cake comes out clean. Once the cake is baked, remove it from the oven and leave it to cool completely in the tin.

Once the cake is cool, make the coffee buttercream. Put the butter in a bowl and add the icing sugar, then beat it well together until light and fluffy using either a wooden spoon, hand-held electric whisk or a stand mixer. Mix in the coffee essence or cooled coffee and beat again until smooth.

Using a palette knife, spread the buttercream all over the top of the traybake. Cut the cake into eight equal-sized pieces, then place the walnuts on top and serve.

180g butter, softened

50g crème fraiche

180g soft light brown sugar

3 eggs

180g wholemeal or regular self-raising flour

½ tsp baking powder

1 tsp Camp coffee essence (or 2 tsp instant coffee mixed with 2 tsp hot water, cooled)

80g shelled walnuts, chopped, plus 40g extra to decorate

For the coffee buttercream

100g unsalted butter, softened

200g icing sugar

½ tsp Camp coffee essence (or 1 tsp instant coffee mixed with 1 tsp hot water, cooled)

Equipment

20cm square cake tin

stand mixer or hand-held electric whisk (optional)

CUPCAKES, MUFFINS & MINI CAKES

RED VELVET CUPCAKES WITH CREAM CHEESE FROSTING

People go wild for my red velvet recipes on social media. I think there's something very special about red velvet cupcakes – it might be their super-rich red colour, or it might be the sweet and slight sourness of the cream cheese frosting. Either way, when you serve these cupcakes, they are always going to be a big hit.

Preheat the oven to 180°C (fan 160°C/350°F/gas 4) and line the cupcake tin with twelve paper cases.

Put the butter and sugar in a bowl and cream them together. The best way to do this is by using a hand-held electric whisk or a stand mixer, but you can use a wooden spoon if you like by squishing the mixture on the sides of the bowl and then beating it hard – it does take longer, but it will work just as well.

The creamed mixture should turn a little paler in colour. Add the sour cream, two of the eggs and half of the flour and beat well until just combined. Add the other two eggs and the rest of the flour and the cocoa powder along with the bicarbonate of soda and food colouring, and mix enough so that everything is just combined – if you over-mix it, the cupcakes may become a little tough, but will still taste good.

Using a large spoon or mechanical ice-cream scoop, divide the mixture between the cases, using a spatula to ensure you get every last bit out of the bowl. Place the tin on the middle shelf of the oven and bake for 25–30 minutes, or until the cupcakes smell baked and are springy to the touch. To check that they are cooked, insert a skewer into the centre of a cupcake – it should come out clean. Once baked, remove the cakes from the oven and leave them to cool down completely.

While the cupcakes are cooling, make the frosting. Put the butter and cream cheese into a bowl with the icing sugar and vanilla and mix together just enough to combine. Use as few stirs as possible – if the cream cheese is over-mixed, the frosting can become too runny. If it does go runny, pop it into the fridge for 10–15 minutes, or until it has firmed up a little. Spoon or pipe the cream cheese frosting over the cupcakes to serve. I like to pipe pretty rosettes on the cakes using the piping bag.

180g butter, softened

180g soft light brown sugar

3 tbsp full-fat sour cream

4 eggs

200g self-raising flour

20g cocoa powder

½ tsp bicarbonate of soda

about ½ tsp red food colouring (use more if you want it super red – I use Sugarflair)

For the frosting

75g butter, softened

50g full-fat cream cheese

250g icing sugar

seeds of ½ vanilla pod or 1 tsp vanilla extract

Equipment

12-hole cupcake tin

hand-held electric whisk or stand mixer (optional)

mechanical ice-cream scoop (optional)

piping bag with 2cm nozzle (optional)

BLACK FOREST GATEAU CUPCAKES WITH MORELLO JAM FILLING

This is a dessert from the '70s made into a modern cupcake for 2017. The cupcake is soaked in Kirsch syrup, but it is fine to leave out the alcohol if you prefer. Choose cherries with intact stalks for more of a dramatic effect. **PICTURED ON PAGE 53.**

Preheat the oven to 180°C (fan 160°C/350°F/gas 4) and line the cupcake tin with twelve paper cases.

First make the cupcakes – this is a super easy sponge to make! Put the crème fraiche, butter, eggs, caster sugar, flour and cocoa powder into a bowl and mix together until well combined. Use as few stirs as possible to give you much lighter, fluffier cupcakes. Then using a large spoon or mechanical ice-cream scoop, divide the mixture between the cases, using a spatula to ensure you get every last bit out of the bowl. Bake in the oven for 15–20 minutes, or until the cupcakes are well risen and smell baked. To check that they are cooked, insert a skewer into the centre of a cupcake – it should come out clean.

As the cupcakes are baking, make the soaking syrup. Put the caster sugar, water and Kirsch, if using, into a small pan over a gentle heat and cook gently until the sugar has dissolved. Increase the heat and allow to bubble for 1 minute, then remove from the heat and set aside to cool a little.

Once the cupcakes are cooked, remove them from the oven and allow to cool for a few minutes in the tin. Then using a melon baller or an apple corer, scoop out the centre of each cupcake, making sure you don't go all the way down to the bottom. Reserve the scooped out bits, and then fill each hole with 1 heaped teaspoon of the cherry jam. Put the reserved cupcake bits back on top and press down to secure, then brush with as much of the Kirsch syrup as you like and set aside while you make the frosting.

Put the cream into a bowl with the icing sugar and vanilla and whisk using the hand-held electric whisk until the cream is just holding its shape with soft peaks. Avoid over-whisking the cream, so it stays smooth, shiny and supple. Spoon or pipe the frosting over the cupcakes, scatter over the grated chocolate and place a cherry on top of each one to serve.

160g crème fraiche

110g butter, softened

4 eggs

220g caster sugar

180g self-raising flour

40g cocoa powder (sifted if lumpy)

125g Morello cherry jam

50g dark chocolate, grated

12 fresh cherries

For the soaking syrup

100g caster sugar

80ml water

3–4 tsp Kirsch (optional)

For the frosting

300ml double cream, well chilled

60g icing sugar

seeds of ½ vanilla pod or 1 tsp of vanilla extract

Equipment

12-hole cupcake tin

mechanical ice-cream scoop (optional)

hand-held electric whisk

piping bag with 1.5cm nozzle (optional)

SPICED BANANA & PINEAPPLE CUPCAKES WITH CRUNCHY COCONUT TOPPING

These cupcakes are also known as 'hummingbird cupcakes' in the States. At first I thought they were named after my old workplace, the Hummingbird Bakery in London, but I've since been told that the name is just a happy coincidence. All of the sponge ingredients go into the bowl together – no creaming or folding, just throw it all in and mix. Easy as pie! **PICTURED ON PAGE 53.**

100g large coconut flakes

180g pineapple

2 large ripe bananas

250g plain flour

2 tsp baking powder

2 tsp ground cinnamon

60g pecan nuts, chopped

175ml sunflower oil

180g soft light brown sugar

2 eggs

For the frosting

50g butter, softened

50g icing sugar

125g full-fat cream cheese

seeds of ½ vanilla pod or 1 tsp vanilla extract

Equipment

12-hole cupcake tin

hand-held electric whisk or stand mixer (optional)

mechanical ice-cream scoop (optional)

piping bag with 2cm nozzle (optional)

Preheat the oven to 180°C (fan 160°C/350°F/gas 4) and line the cupcake tin with twelve paper cases.

Put the coconut flakes on a baking tray and place them in the oven for 2–3 minutes, until the coconut flakes are going golden brown. Keep an eye on the flakes as they can catch pretty quickly. When they have changed colour, remove from the oven and set aside to cool.

Roughly mash up the pineapple in a bowl, discarding excess juice, then mash up the bananas in another bowl.

Put the flour, baking powder, cinnamon, pecan nuts, sunflower oil, sugar, mashed banana, mashed pineapple and eggs into a large bowl and mix it together using a hand-held electric whisk or a stand mixer until it is all combined. You can also do this by hand using a wooden spoon.

Using a large spoon or mechanical ice-cream scoop, divide the combined mixture between the paper cases, using a spatula to ensure you get every last bit out of the bowl. Bake the cupcakes for 25–30 minutes, or until they smell baked and are springy to the touch. To check that they are cooked, insert a skewer into the centre of a cupcake – it should come out clean. Once baked, remove the cakes from the oven and leave them to cool down completely.

While the cupcakes are cooling, make the cream cheese frosting. Put the butter and icing sugar together in a bowl and beat well using a wooden spoon until light and fluffy. Add the cream cheese and vanilla and stir together just enough for it to be nicely combined. Don't over-whisk it at this stage otherwise it can get a bit too runny. Spoon or pipe the cream cheese frosting over the cupcakes, and then sprinkle the coconut flakes on top making sure that they completely cover the frosting. Serve.

BANANA & COFFEE-CRUMB CUPCAKES

This cupcake is based on a yeasted German cake that has a sponge base and a crumble-like topping. This kind of cake has many varieties and is often known as 'coffee cake' stateside, not necessarily because it contains coffee, but because it's intended to be eaten alongside a cup of coffee! Confused? I was at first! Change the crumble topping if you like by using some finely chopped walnuts or pecan nuts in place of the bananas.

Preheat the oven to 180°C (fan 160°C/350°F/gas 4) and line the cupcake tin with twelve paper cases.

First make the crumb. Put the caster sugar, butter, flour and salt into a bowl. Using your thumb and your fingers, pick up bits of the mixture, rub it together and then let it fall back into the bowl. Keep doing this until the mixture resembles breadcrumbs, then squeeze some of the breadcrumb bits together to make slightly larger lumps. It is good to do this as it helps ensure that the crumb is nicely mixed in and the larger bits give the cakes an even better texture. Set the crumb aside.

To make the cupcakes, cream together the butter and the soft light brown sugar in a large bowl until the mixture goes lighter and fluffier. It won't go super light as brown sugar does not go as fluffy as white sugar. Add two of the eggs with half of the flour and mix well to combine. Then add the other egg with the rest of the flour, the sour cream, baking powder and coffee essence and mix it together, using as few stirs as possible to give you light cupcakes.

Using a large spoon or mechanical ice-cream scoop, divide the mixture between the cases, using a spatula to ensure you get every last bit out of the bowl.

Peel the bananas and cut them into thin slices. Arrange three slices on top of each cupcake, and then sprinkle over an even layer of the crumb and bake in the oven for about 20 minutes, or until the cupcakes smell baked and are well risen. To check that they are cooked, insert a skewer into the centre of a cupcake – it should come out clean. Once the cupcakes are cooked, remove them from the oven and allow to cool a little in the tin.

Give the cupcakes a light dusting of icing sugar and serve warm with a nice cup of coffee.

200g butter, softened

180g soft light brown sugar

3 eggs

220g plain or wholemeal flour

3 tbsp sour cream

1 tsp baking powder

3 tbsp Camp coffee essence

2 just ripe bananas

icing sugar, for dusting

For the crumb

35g caster sugar

35g butter, cold and cut into small cubes

70g plain flour

pinch of salt

Equipment

12-hole cupcake tin

mechanical ice-cream scoop (optional)

MAPLE WALNUT CRUMBLE MUFFINS

I occasionally make these for brunch at the weekend, although they are more like a cake than something that should be eaten for breakfast! It is quite honestly difficult not to eat the whole lot in one go. You could use honey instead of maple syrup if you don't have it in your cupboard, but I do love the more subtle and toasty flavours of a good maple syrup.

180ml buttermilk or 180ml whole milk and juice of ½ lemon

275g self-raising flour

small pinch of salt

1 tsp bicarbonate of soda

70g soft light brown sugar

125g walnuts, roughly chopped

130ml sunflower oil

50ml maple syrup

2 eggs

For the crumble topping

50g plain flour

pinch of salt

35g butter, cold and cut into cubes

35g soft light brown sugar

½ tsp ground cinnamon (optional)

Equipment

12-hole muffin tin

food processor (optional)

mechanical ice-cream scoop (optional)

Preheat the oven to 180°C (fan 160°C/350°F/gas 4) and line the muffin tin with twelve paper cases. If you're making your own buttermilk, put the milk and lemon juice in a jug and allow it to sit for 15 minutes.

Next, make the crumble topping. Put the plain flour, salt, butter and sugar into a food processor along with the cinnamon, if using, and pulse it all together for about 15 seconds until the mixture resembles breadcrumbs. You could also put all of the crumble topping ingredients into a bowl and rub them together with your fingertips, letting the mixture fall back into the bowl. Keep doing this until the mixture resembles breadcrumbs and then set aside.

To make the muffins, put the self-raising flour, salt, bicarbonate of soda and sugar into a bowl with the walnuts and mix to combine with a spatula. Add the sunflower oil, maple syrup, eggs and buttermilk and mix it together, using as few stirs as possible until just combined to give you light and fluffy muffins. If you over-mix it, the muffins may become a little tough, but will still taste good. Then using a large spoon or mechanical ice-cream scoop, divide the mixture between the cases, using a spatula to ensure you get every last bit out of the bowl.

Sprinkle an even layer of the crumble topping over each muffin and bake in the oven for 18–20 minutes, or until the muffins are cooked through. To check that they are cooked, insert a skewer into the centre of a muffin – it should come out clean. Once cooked, remove from the oven and allow to cool a little in the tin. These muffins are best served warm, but are also delicious cold.

I like to pop these muffins in the freezer in an airtight container. When I need one, I can just take it out of the freezer the night before to thaw out – or give it a blast in the microwave so I can eat it straightaway!

DEVIL'S FOOD CUPCAKE CONES

Devil's food cake is a very rich chocolate cake, made with cocoa powder and melted dark chocolate. It makes a delicious surprise filling for these ice-cream themed cupcakes. I recommend piping the cake mixture into the ice-cream cones because it's quick and ensures you get the mixture right to the bottom. Decorate with your favourite ice-cream toppings – I've used sprinkles, but you may prefer finely chopped nuts.

Preheat the oven to 180°C (fan 160°C/350°F/gas 4) and sit the ice-cream cones in the holes of the cupcake tin to hold them upright.

Melt the butter in a small pan over a low heat, and then take the pan off the heat and add the dark chocolate. Leave the chocolate to melt.

Lightly beat the eggs. Put the flour, cocoa powder, sugar, bicarbonate of soda, eggs and salt in a large bowl with the melted butter and chocolate mixture. Mix to just combine with the hand-held electric whisk and spoon the batter into the disposable piping bag. Snip off the end to give you a wide hole, and then pipe into the ice-cream cones, filling them no more than three-quarters full or they will overflow while they are cooking.

Place the tin into the oven and bake for 20–25 minutes, or until they are baked. To check that they are cooked, insert a skewer into the centre of a cupcake cone – it should come out clean. Once the cupcake cones are baked, remove them from the oven and leave to cool completely.

While the cones are cooling, make the frosting. Put all of the ingredients apart from the colouring into a large bowl and beat well with the hand-held electric whisk or until the mixture goes light and fluffy. You can also use a stand mixer fitted with a paddle attachment to do this. To colour the frosting, divide it into bowls and stir through each food colouring, as desired.

Take a piping bag fitted with the 1cm straight nozzle and half-fill it with the frosting. If you have coloured your frosting, use a different bag for each colour. Pipe the frosting onto the cupcakes so that it looks like ice cream, as per the photograph opposite.

Add sprinkles to each one, and if you feel like it, stick half a chocolate flake in the top to make it look like our beloved Mr Whippy! Serve.

Ingredients

12 flat-bottomed cones

160g butter

40g dark chocolate, roughly chopped

2 large eggs

160g self-raising flour

40g cocoa powder

160g caster sugar

½ tsp bicarbonate of soda

pinch of salt

2–3 tbsp sprinkles

6 chocolate flakes, cut in half (optional)

For the frosting

150g butter, softened

350g icing sugar

seeds of 1 vanilla pod or 2 tsp vanilla extract

few drops each of blue and pink food colouring (optional)

Equipment

12-hole cupcake tin

hand-held electric whisk or stand mixer

disposable piping bag

2 x piping bags with 1cm straight nozzles

RASPBERRY, ALMOND & VANILLA BUNS

This is paying homage to my first ever recipe – the one that opened my eyes to baking. Once a term at primary school, aged 5, we would have a cooking lesson with Mrs Tutton. My mother would get all the ingredients ready for me in an old tin, with each component carefully wrapped in cling film. The night before I would be beside myself looking forward to the baking fest, and wouldn't be able to sleep!

Preheat the oven to 180°C (fan 160°C/350°F/gas 4) and line a large baking sheet with baking parchment.

Put the flour, almonds, baking powder and butter into a bowl and then rub the mixture together using your thumb and fingers. Simply pick up bits of the mixture, rub it and then let it fall back into the bowl. Keep doing this until the mixture resembles fine breadcrumbs. Stir in the sugar, then using a wooden spoon, make a well in the centre of the bowl and add the egg and vanilla and stir this all together. Then put your hands in the bowl and squidge the mixture together. If the mixture is a little dry, add 2–3 tablespoons of warm water to bring it together.

Put heaped tablespoons of the mixture onto the lined baking sheet, being sure to leave enough room for them to spread out. You should have enough mixture for about sixteen buns.

Using a floured finger or the end of the wooden spoon, make a dent in the top of each bun and spoon in a teaspoon of the raspberry jam. Pop the sheet into the oven and bake for 15 minutes, or until the buns are cooked through and turning a light golden brown around the edges.

Once the buns are baked, remove them from the oven and top up each bun with a little more raspberry jam, then leave to cool. This is the bit I always find the hardest, and have always found the hardest: leaving the buns to cool down enough to be eaten. Most of the time I just had to dig in the moment they came out of the oven, which would always result in me burning my tongue a little on the super-hot raspberry jam!

180g self-raising flour

40g ground almonds

pinch of baking powder

110g butter, cut into cubes

110g caster sugar

1 egg

seeds of ½ vanilla pod or ½ tsp vanilla extract

6 tbsp seedless raspberry jam

MERINGUE-TOPPED CUPCAKES WITH LEMON & RASPBERRY FILLING

These little cakes are tasty and oh-so pretty. I can't get enough of lemon and lime – they are some of my favourite flavours when it comes to baking. You can fill your little cakes with homemade lemon curd (see page 278) or you can just buy some shop-bought stuff. If you are doing the latter then go for the organic one if you can, as it makes such a difference to the final flavour.

150g unsalted butter, softened, plus a little for greasing

150g caster sugar

3 eggs

150g plain flour

7.5g baking powder

For the filling

75g lemon curd (see page 278)

12 equal-sized raspberries

For the Swiss meringue

120g egg whites

240g caster sugar

Equipment

12-hole cupcake tin

stand mixer or hand-held electric whisk

sugar thermometer

kitchen blowtorch

Preheat the oven to 180°C (fan 160°C/350°F/gas 4) and make sure the shelf in the middle of the oven is at the ready. Line the cupcake tin with twelve paper cases.

Put the butter and sugar together in a bowl and whisk well until it goes pale using a wooden spoon, stand mixer or hand-held electric whisk. Then add one of the eggs with half of the flour and all of the baking powder and mix together until just combined. Then add the remaining two eggs and flour and mix again until combined. If you are using a stand mixer then use the paddle attachment and be sure to scrape the bowl down between each addition to make sure that everything is nicely mixed in.

Divide the mixture between the twelve paper cases and smooth the tops with the back of a spoon. Pop the cakes in the oven to bake for about 15 minutes. Meanwhile, if you are making the lemon curd from scratch, make it and set it aside to cool down.

To check that the cakes are cooked, insert a skewer into the centre of one – it should come out clean. Once the cakes are baked, remove them from the oven and leave them to cool down completely.

Using a melon baller or an apple corer, scoop out the centre of each cupcake, making sure you don't go all the way down to the bottom. Reserve the scooped out bits, and then fill each hole with about ½ teaspoon of the lemon curd followed by a raspberry. Top with another ½ teaspoon of the lemon curd, and place the reserved piece of sponge on top and set aside.

Next, make the meringue. Pour about 5cm of cold water into a medium pan and choose a large bowl that will sit comfortably on top.

>

MERINGUE-TOPPED CUPCAKES WITH LEMON & RASPBERRY FILLING

Bring the water to the boil. Off the heat, whisk the egg whites and sugar in the bowl by hand until they become light and frothy.

Reduce the heat to simmer the water and then pop the bowl on top. With the sugar thermometer to hand, continue to whisk the mixture, stopping to check the temperature occasionally. The temperature needs to reach 70°C (160°F).

Once it has reached the correct temperature, remove the bowl from the heat and whisk the meringue on high for 10 minutes, or until the mixture has cooled down to body temperature, increased in volume and is glossy with stiff peaks.

Spoon a heaped tablespoon of the meringue onto the top of a cupcake and use the tip of the spoon to shape it into a nice peak. Repeat with the remaining cupcakes and meringue, arranging them on a baking sheet as you go. Then, take the kitchen blowtorch and lightly toast the sides of the meringue with it. Serve.

You can tell if your meringue is ready by lifting some up on the end of your whisk – the meringue should stand straight up. Some people say to hold the bowl over your head. If it doesn't fall out, it's ready!

BLUEBERRY, DATE & OAT
MUFFINS WITH YOGHURT

I find that using sugar and dates together in this recipe provides the best depth of flavour. The yoghurt lightens the crumb a little and gives a small amount of sourness, which is enhanced by using the buttermilk or soured milk. Instead of the blueberries, feel free to use your favourite berries, such as raspberries or blackberries – or use a mixture of them all to make a summer berry muffin.

Preheat the oven to 180°C (fan 160°C/350°F/gas 4) and line the muffin tin with twelve paper cases. If you're making your own buttermilk, put the milk and lemon juice in a jug and allow it to sit for 15 minutes.

Put the flour, bicarbonate of soda, cinnamon, sugar and dates into a large bowl and stir to combine. Then add the melted butter along with the egg, yoghurt and buttermilk, using as few stirs as possible to produce lighter, fluffier muffins. Fold in the blueberries until just combined.

Using a large spoon or mechanical ice-cream scoop, divide the mixture between the cases, using a spatula to ensure you get every last bit out of the bowl. Waste not want not! Sprinkle the oats on top and bake for 20–25 minutes, until the muffins are cooked through. To check that they are cooked, insert a skewer into the centre of a muffin – it should come out clean.

Once the muffins are baked, remove them from the oven and leave to cool a little in the tin. They are delicious served warm or cold.

100ml buttermilk or 100ml whole milk and juice of ¼ lemon

240g self-raising flour

½ tsp bicarbonate of soda

½–1 tsp of ground cinnamon

150g soft light brown sugar

180g pitted dates, finely chopped (Medjool or any sticky soft date)

90g butter, melted

1 egg

200g Greek yoghurt

75g blueberries

50g porridge oats

Equipment

12-hole muffin tin

mechanical ice-cream scoop (optional)

64 CUPCAKES, MUFFINS & MINI CAKES

BROWN SUGAR &
SPICE ROCK BUNS

Is this one of the first things you ever baked? The rock bun seems rooted in many people's baking memories. Use whichever dried fruit you like – you could even soak the dried fruit in alcohol or apple juice overnight to add some extra flavour and help to keep them nice and moist.

Preheat the oven to 180°C (fan 160°C/350°F/gas 4) and line two baking sheets with baking parchment.

Put the flour, baking powder, mixed spice and butter into a bowl. Using your thumb and your fingers, pick up bits of the mixture, rub it together and then let it fall back into the bowl until the mixture resembles fine breadcrumbs. If you like, you can pop the mixture into the food processor and blitz until it resembles fine breadcrumbs.

If you have used a food processor, tip the mixture into a mixing bowl. Add the vanilla, sugar, and your choice of dried fruit to the mixture and stir together to combine using a wooden spoon. Then add the eggs and the egg white and mix again to form a fairly tight dough.

Using a large spoon or a mechanical ice-cream scoop, divide the mixture into twelve equal-sized blobs on the lined baking sheets. Sprinkle each one with a little extra brown sugar and then place them in the oven and bake for 15–20 minutes, or until the buns are firm and golden brown.

Once the rock buns are cooked, remove them from the oven and leave to cool completely on the baking sheets before serving.

250g plain flour

2 tsp baking powder

1 tsp mixed spice

125g butter, cold and cut into cubes

seeds of ½ vanilla pod or 1 tsp vanilla extract

80g soft light brown sugar, plus extra for sprinkling over the top

150g raisins or dried cranberries or mixed dried fruit, chopped

2 eggs

1 egg white

Equipment

food processor (optional)

mechanical ice-cream scoop (optional)

Using a food processor to make the mixture takes less time but I prefer to do it by hand – mainly so I don't have to wash the whole machine and blade, which is definitely not my favourite part of baking!

MINI RASPBERRY SWIRL CHEESECAKES

These are the perfect dinner party dessert, as you can make them the day before you plan to serve – I find it makes for a much more relaxing evening when I've prepared stuff in advance and can focus on my guests. I like to make these with raspberries, but it could be fun to try them with cranberries or blueberries. If you do decide to experiment then please let me know how you get on through my social media!

25g butter

10 digestive biscuits

For the filling

600g full-fat cream cheese

190g caster sugar

seeds of ½ vanilla pod or 1 tsp vanilla extract

3 eggs

For the raspberry swirl

120g raspberries

1 heaped tbsp caster sugar

Equipment

12-hole cupcake tin

food processor

Preheat the oven to 160°C (fan 140°C/325°/gas 3). Line the cupcake tin with twelve paper cases and set aside.

Melt the butter in a small pan or in the microwave. Leave to cool a little. Put the digestive biscuits into the food processor and blitz until they resemble breadcrumbs and then tip them into a bowl. Add the melted butter and mix to combine and then divide the mixture between the paper cases, pressing each one down super well so it is packed tight.

To make the filling, put the cream cheese, sugar, vanilla and eggs into a large bowl and mix until just combined. This mixture does not need to be beaten but just mixed together. Divide it between the biscuit bases and set aside.

Put the raspberries in a food processor and blitz until smooth, then place a sieve over a bowl and push the raspberry puree through the sieve to get rid of the seeds. Discard the seeds and then add enough of the caster sugar to taste. The amount of sugar you will need depends on how sweet the raspberries are, so taste them as you add the sugar and see how you go.

Using a spoon, put blobs of the puree onto each cheesecake and then take a skewer and drag the blobs outwards to create a swirl pattern. Place the cheesecakes in the oven and bake for 18–20 minutes, or until the cheesecakes are just set but still have a slight wobble in the centre.

Once cooked, remove from the oven and leave to cool completely, then place in the fridge to chill. I usually take the cheesecakes out of the fridge about 20 minutes before serving, so that they are not super cold for the guests to eat. Enjoy!

PEANUT BUTTER & STRAWBERRY FINANCIERS

It is best to make financier cakes just before you want to eat them. They are such a pretty shape, made with moulds you can buy online. I have based this recipe flavouring on the classic American combination of peanut butter and jelly – you can of course use different fruit but I think that strawberry is a perfect match.

Preheat the oven to 180°C (fan 160°C/350°F/gas 4) and spray the financier mould sheets with oil. I have flexible financier moulds, and I like to put them on a baking sheet as this makes it easier to move them in and out of the oven.

Put the butter into a small pan over a low heat and cook, stirring all the time so that the milk solids in the butter, which cook faster than the rest of the butter, are evenly distributed. Keep on cooking for about 3–5 minutes, or until the butter starts to smell nutty and turn a medium brown. Pour the melted butter into a medium bowl, stir in the peanut butter until well combined and set aside.

Put the sugar, flour and ground almonds together in another bowl and stir them together. Add the egg whites, whisking so that everything is well combined, and then add one third of this egg-white mixture to the butter mixture and stir to combine. This step loosens up the peanut butter mixture a little so that both mixtures combine together more easily in the next step.

Tip the butter mixture back into the sugar, flour and ground almond mixture, mixing well to combine. Spoon the mixture into the piping bag, snip about 1.5cm off the end of the bag and then pipe the mixture between the moulds. You can also use a jug to do this if you prefer.

Place the financiers in the oven and bake for 18–20 minutes, until the financiers are baked through, springy to the touch and are a light golden-brown colour. When they are cooked, remove them from the oven and set aside to cool.

When the financiers have cooled, gently remove them from the moulds and place them on a serving plate. Put half a teaspoon of the strawberry jam on top of each one along with a slice of strawberry. Sprinkle over some icing sugar if you like, and serve.

oil, for spraying

170g butter

80g smooth peanut butter

300g caster sugar

35g plain flour

200g ground almonds

270g egg whites

To decorate

5 tbsp strawberry jam, seedless

4–5 strawberries, finely sliced

icing sugar, for dusting (optional)

Equipment

2 x 12-hole financier mould sheets, each mould 7 x 2.5cm in size and 3cm deep

disposable piping bag (optional)

BROWN BUTTER, BROWN SUGAR FRENCH MADELEINES

These shell-shaped treats are very special and are best served warm – top restaurants bake them to order and serve them fresh from the oven. Allow time for careful whisking and folding to make these light and buttery; the process is easy, but just takes a little patience. Some recipes include baking powder to ensure the cakes get a good rise, but these are just lovely without it. You can make these savoury by adding a little thyme or rosemary with the flour.

Preheat the oven to 180°C (fan 160°C/350°F/gas 4) and spray the madeleine tins with a little oil. If you don't have three tins, you can bake the madeleines in batches, keeping the mixture in the fridge when you are not using it.

Put the soft brown sugar into a food processor, blitz it until it is really fine and then set it aside. Place the butter in a small pan over a low heat and cook it until it melts. Then turn up the heat and continue to cook until the butter goes golden brown and starts to smell nutty. Take it off the heat and allow it to cool down a little.

It is best to whisk the eggs first and then add the sugar rather than whisking it all at once as this will give you much more volume. Put the eggs into a bowl with the salt and whisk them up until they are really light and fluffy. The best way to do this is by using a hand-held electric whisk or a stand mixer. It can take the mixture up to 10 minutes to get super light and fluffy – this stage does take a little time, but it is so worth it. The mixture is ready when it is mousse-like and reaches the ribbon stage.

Add the blitzed sugar and the vanilla into the bowl, tipping it around the outside of the egg mixture so that you don't knock out all of the valuable air you have whisked into it. Then whisk this up again so that it goes back to being super light and fluffy. Keep whisking it again until it becomes mousse-like and reaches the ribbon stage once more – this can take another good 10 minutes, but it is worth taking your time for your lovely madeleines.

oil, for spraying

100g soft light brown sugar

85g butter

4 eggs

small pinch of salt

seeds of ½ vanilla pod or 1 tsp vanilla extract

100g plain flour, sifted (or plain gluten-free flour from Doves Farm)

icing sugar, for dusting (optional)

Equipment

3 x 12-hole madeleine tins, each mould 5 x 7.5cm in size

food processor

hand-held electric whisk or stand mixer

disposable piping bag (optional)

To check the mixture has reached the ribbon stage, lift up some of the mixture on the whisk and let it fall back down – it should sit on the surface of the mixture for 6–8 seconds or so before slowly disappearing back in.

Pour the melted butter into the bowl, tipping it around the outside of the mixture, as before. This time, fold the mixture together with a spatula, using as few stirs as possible to keep the air in. Gently tip the flour into the bowl, again tipping it around the outside of the batter, and then fold it in to combine with the spatula.

Spoon the well-combined mixture into the piping bag, snip about 1.5cm off the end of the bag and then pipe the mixture between the moulds until they are level, leaving 1–2mm of space from the top for the mixture to rise. You can also use a large spoon instead of the piping bag, if you prefer, leaving 1–2mm of space from the top for the madeleines to rise.

Pop the tins into the oven and bake the madeleines for about 10–12 minutes, or until they are a light golden-brown colour and are springy to the touch.

Once the madeleines are baked, remove them from the oven and carefully loosen them from the tins with a palette knife. Serve immediately, pretty 'scalloped'-side up (top-side down). Dust with some icing sugar, if you fancy it.

Flour is heavy and has a habit of sinking, so when you add it to the mixture, make sure you dig deep into the bottom of the bowl to mix it all in. I like to use a spatula to do this, so I can really scoop and scrape into the bottom of the bowl.

PUFF PASTRY ECCLES CAKES

Some say these layered pastries should be made with flaky pastry and others prefer puff pastry. I've opted for puff, because it gives a more refined look. You can make your own puff pastry, if you like (see page 271). Alternatively you can buy ready-prepared all-butter or a low-fat puff – both work equally well, but the all-butter puff has more natural flavour. If you're buying puff pastry, always avoid the ready-rolled version, which I find is rolled out too thinly.

Sprinkle some flour on a work surface and then roll out the puff pastry until it is about 5mm thick. It needs to be just big enough to cut out eight circles, each 10cm across – check by holding up the cutter. When you are happy that it is rolled to the right size, use the 10cm cutter to stamp out eight puff pastry circles and arrange them on a baking sheet. Pop the pastry into the fridge to rest for at least 10–15 minutes while you make the filling.

Put the melted butter into a bowl with rest of the filling ingredients, and then mix it all together. Take the pastry from the fridge and place 1 tablespoon of the mixture into the centre of each circle. Gather the pastry around the filling to enclose and squeeze it together, then flip it over so the top is facing upwards and gently pat it into a smooth round. Flatten a little more with the palm of your hand into an oval that's about 7.5 x 6cm in size, and then place it onto the baking sheet. Repeat with the rest of the rounds and then put them in the fridge for 10–15 minutes to firm up.

Preheat the oven to 200°C (fan 180°C/400°F/gas 6). After the cakes have firmed up, make three little slashes in the top of each one using a small, very sharp knife. Brush the cakes all over with the beaten egg to glaze.

Mix together the demerara sugar and cinnamon and sprinkle a little bit over each Eccles cake, then bake them in the oven for 15–20 minutes, or until the pastry is puffed up and golden brown.

Remove the cakes from the oven. I love to eat them while they are still a little warm with a cup of tea, but they are also great cold. Be super careful when you eat these warm, as the fruit filling gets silly hot in the oven. I am told that these go down very well with a nice strong cheese – I am yet to try that combination though!

1 quantity puff pastry (page 271) or 500g packet shop-bought puff pastry

plain flour, for dusting

For the filling

1 tbsp melted butter

60g soft light brown sugar

180g mixed dried fruit

50g mixed peel

½ tsp ground cinnamon

½ tsp ground ginger

zest of 1 orange (optional)

To decorate

1 egg, lightly beaten

1 tbsp demerara sugar

½ tsp ground cinnamon

Equipment

10cm straight-sided round cookie cutter

ENGLISH BUTTERMILK
WHOLEMEAL SPELT MUFFINS

As delectable as they may be, American muffins have totally overshadowed the classic English muffin of late. The only way to find them is in a large packet from the supermarket, so I much prefer to make them. Let's bring back the English breakfast staple: English muffins slathered in butter and jam! I am using a mixture of wholemeal and white spelt flour, but you could use regular plain flour if you can't find spelt flour.

If you're making your own buttermilk, put the milk and lemon juice in a jug and allow it to sit for 10–15 minutes. Put both the flours in a bowl with the yeast, sugar and salt.

Make a well in the centre and pour in the warm water and buttermilk and use a wooden spoon to mix everything together. Place the dough on a floured work surface, and knead it for 10 minutes by hand or 5 minutes in a stand mixer fitted with a dough hook attachment. To check that the dough has been kneaded enough, pick the dough up and then fold the outer edges of it underneath to make a ball with a nice taut top. Then cover your finger with flour and prod the side of the dough, making an indent about 5mm deep – the dough should spring back all the way if it has been kneaded enough.

Place the dough into a clean bowl and spray it with a little oil, then cover with cling film, so that it is airtight but not taut, giving the dough space to rise. Leave in a warm, but not hot, place to rise for about an hour. After an hour, remove the cling film, make another 5mm indent in the dough. The dough should spring back but only halfway this time. If it does not spring back and just stays there, then it needs a little more time.

Preheat the oven to 200°C (fan 180°C/400°F/gas 6). Remove the dough from the bowl and lightly dust the work surface with a little flour. Roll it out to a 1.5cm thickness, and then cut out muffins with the cutter, re-rolling leftover dough until you get thirteen muffins.

Put half of the muffins in a large non-stick frying pan over a medium heat (or how many can fit into your frying pan with a bit of space around them so they cook quickly) and cook them for 3 minutes on each side, or until trademark brown. Transfer them to a large baking tray and repeat with the rest of the muffins, and then put into the oven for 10–12 minutes, or until well risen and cooked through. Serve immediately with butter and jam or leave to cool.

210ml buttermilk, or 210ml whole milk and juice of ¼ lemon

300g white spelt flour, plus extra for dusting

275g wholemeal spelt flour

7g sachet fast action dried yeast

1 tsp soft light brown sugar

1 tsp salt

175ml warm water

oil, for spraying

Equipment

stand mixer (optional)

8cm straight-sided round cookie cutter

SAGE, ROSEMARY & BLACK PEPPER MADELEINES

MAKES 36

These savoury madeleines make a nice alternative to bread for a special occasion, and they can also be great as canapés. Use the base of the recipe to experiment with other herbs if you like. You could remove the sage and/or rosemary and use things like thyme, marjoram or chives instead, or sprinkle the savoury cakes with freshly grated Parmesan cheese before you bake them.

Preheat the oven to 180°C (fan 160°C/350°F/gas 4) and spray the 12-hole madeleine tins with a little oil. If you don't have three tins, you can bake the cakes in batches, keeping the batter in the fridge when you are not using it. Melt the butter in a small pan or in the microwave and leave to cool a little.

Whisk the eggs until they are really light and fluffy, using a hand-held electric whisk or a stand mixer fitted with a whisk attachment. It can take a good 10 minutes to get the eggs light, fluffy and mousse-like. Then add the sugar, making sure that you pour the sugar around the outside of the eggs so that you don't knock out the air you have whisked into it. Whisk this up again until light and fluffy – this take another good 8–10 minutes. To check the mixture has reached the ribbon stage, lift up some of the mixture on the whisk and let it fall back down – it should sit on the surface of the mixture for 6–8 seconds or so before slowly disappearing back in.

When the mixture is ready, pour the melted butter into the bowl and then add the salt, black pepper and rosemary. Using a spatula, carefully fold everything in to combine, keeping in as much air as possible. Then add the flour, again folding it all in, being sure to mix in the flour that falls right to the bottom of the bowl with the spatula. Carefully divide the mixture between the prepared tins so that they are level, leaving 1–2mm space from the top to allow them to rise. Gently lay a sage leaf on each madeleine.

Bake the madeleines in the oven for 10–12 minutes, or until they are golden brown and springy to the touch. Then remove them from the oven and leave to cool for a minute before very gently easing them out of the tins with a palette knife. Leave to cool slightly on a wire rack before arranging on a plate to serve. These are best eaten while they are still warm.

oil, for spraying

100g butter

4 eggs

80g caster sugar

pinch of sea salt flakes

2 tsp cracked black pepper

1 tbsp chopped fresh rosemary

100g wholemeal or plain flour

36 small fresh sage leaves (equal in size)

Equipment

3 x 12-hole madeleine tins, each mould 5 x 7.5cm in size

hand-held electric whisk or stand mixer

CHEESE & PANCETTA SCONES WITH THYME AND CHIVES

If I made a list of my top ten foods, I think scones would be on there: so simple but soft, moreish and the taste of home. I like to use a square cutter, but you can use a round one, and by all means change the thyme for dill, coriander or tarragon if you prefer. The volume of liquid for your dough can depend on temperature and how thirsty your flour is, so you may not need to add all of the milk to the mixture – just add most of it and see how you go.

Preheat the oven to 220°C (fan 200°C/425°F/gas 7) and lightly dust a large baking sheet with flour. If you're making your own buttermilk, put the milk and lemon juice in a jug and allow it to sit for 15 minutes.

Fry the pancetta cubes in a small frying pan and over a medium heat until just crisp, then tip them onto some kitchen paper to drain off the excess fat.

Put the flour, baking powder, mustard powder, paprika, if using, and salt into a large bowl with the butter, then pick the mixture up in your hands and rub it together before letting it fall back into the bowl. Repeat this until the mixture resembles fine breadcrumbs. You can also use a food processor to do this.

Stir 150g of the cheese into the butter and flour mixture with the chives, thyme and pancetta and then make a well in the centre of the mixture and add most of the buttermilk. Stir it all together with a round-bladed knife to make a soft, but not sticky dough. You might not need all of the milk, just add most of it and stop when you have a smooth and soft but not sticky dough.

Put your hands in the bowl and bring the mixture together to form a ball. Then using a rolling pin, gently roll out the dough on a lightly floured surface until it is 3cm thick. Using a lightly dusted cutter, stamp out eight scones and place them on the prepared baking sheet. Try not to twist the cutter, otherwise your scones may not have a nice, straight rise. Scrunch up the excess dough, knead very gently until smooth and then re-roll to cut as many scones as possible.

Brush the tops of the scones lightly with milk or buttermilk to glaze and then sprinkle over the remaining 50g of cheese. Place the scones in the oven to cook for 10–12 minutes, or until they are well risen, firm and a nice golden brown with the cheese bubbling on top. Once they are cooked, remove them from the oven and set aside to cool a little before serving with loads of butter.

185ml buttermilk or 185ml whole milk with juice from ½ lemon, plus a little extra for glazing

200g pancetta cubes

360g self-raising flour, plus extra for dusting

1 tsp baking powder

1 tsp English mustard powder

large pinch of paprika (optional)

pinch of sea salt flakes

85g butter, cold and cut into cubes

200g mature Cheddar cheese, grated

15g bunch of fresh chives, finely sliced or snipped

1 heaped tbsp fresh thyme leaves

Equipment

food processor (optional)

8cm straight-sided or fluted square cutter

BREADS

SWEET RICH FAN TANS WITH CINNAMON GINGER TOPPING

It would be lovely to have an emotional attachment to every recipe in this book, but that's not always the case. Sometimes I spot baked goods when I am at a restaurant or farmer's market and I think, 'Ooh, yes ... I like the look of that!' and feel inspired to come home and write a recipe based on whatever has tickled my fancy. This recipe for rich sweet rolls came from such an inspiration. They look fabulous and are just that little bit different.

Melt the butter in a small pan or in the microwave, then set aside to cool a little. Warm the milk in a small pan or in the microwave.

Put the flour into a large bowl and add the salt and maple syrup on one side and the yeast to the other side. Add 4 tablespoons of the melted butter and three-quarters of the warm milk (about 225ml) to the bowl, and then gently move the flour around with your fingertips. Continue to add the remaining milk, a little at a time, until you've picked up all of the flour from the sides of the bowl and the dough is soft but not sticky. Keep checking the texture as you add the milk, as you will probably not need all of it.

Spray the work surface with a little oil, then tip the dough onto it and start kneading. Continue to knead for 5–10 minutes (10 minutes if doing this by hand or 5 minutes if you are using a stand mixer fitted with a dough hook attachment).

To check that the dough has been kneaded enough, pick the dough up and then fold the outer edges of it underneath to make a ball with a nice taut top. Then cover your finger with flour and prod the side of the dough, making an indent about 5mm deep – the dough should spring back all the way if it has been kneaded enough. This shows that the gluten in the dough has been worked enough and is nice and stretchy and ready for the next stage. If it is not quite ready, knead the dough for a few more minutes

When the dough is ready, lightly spray a large bowl with oil. Put the dough into the bowl and cover it with cling film that has also been sprayed with a little oil. The cling film should be airtight but not taut, to give the bread enough room to rise. Leave it in a warm, but not hot, place to rise until it has doubled in size – this will take at least 1 hour but could take longer depending on the temperature of the room.

110g butter

300ml whole milk

500g strong white bread flour, plus extra for dusting

2 tsp fine salt

1 tbsp maple syrup

7g sachet of fast-action dried yeast

oil, for spraying

For the topping

3 tbsp maple syrup

2 tbsp soft light brown sugar

½ tsp ground cinnamon

½ tsp ground ginger

Equipment

stand mixer (optional)

2 x 12-hole muffin tins

>

SWEET RICH FAN TANS WITH CINNAMON GINGER TOPPING

When your dough is ready, drop it onto a lightly floured surface. Then fold it inwards repeatedly until all the air is knocked out and the dough is smooth. Form the dough into an oblong by flattening the dough out slightly, and then roll it out into a square, slightly larger than 40 x 40cm. Brush 2 tablespoons of the melted butter over the dough square.

Using a large sharp knife and a ruler, trim down the square until it is exactly 40cm square and then cut it into ten strips, each 4cm wide. Stack five of the strips on top of each other and set aside. Then stack the five remaining strips on top of each other in another pile, giving you two piles that look exactly the same.

Take one of the stacks and arrange it so the longest side is facing you. Using a sharp knife, cut this stack into eight slices, each 4cm wide. Repeat with the other stack, giving you sixteen little piles of layered bread dough.

Quickly brush the muffin tins with the rest of the melted butter and put one of the dough piles into the hole, cut-side up. Repeat with the rest of the dough piles. Spray cling film lightly with oil and use it to cover the dough, so that it is airtight but not taut to give the dough a little room to rise. Leave the muffin tins in a warm place for about 1 hour or so until the piles have doubled in size and filled out the muffin holes.

Preheat the oven to 200°C (fan 180°C/400°F/gas 6). To prepare the topping, put the maple syrup in a little bowl with a pastry brush in it and set aside, and then mix the soft brown sugar in another small bowl with cinnamon and ginger and also set this aside.

Remove the cling film from the tins and bake the fan tans for 20 minutes, until they are well risen and golden brown. When the fan tans are baked, quickly take them out of the oven and brush them with the maple syrup. Sprinkle each one with some of the spiced sugar mix, then put them back in the oven for a couple of minutes to glaze.

Take the fan tans out of the oven and leave them to cool a little before serving.

When it's time for the fan tans to rise, I usually turn the oven on and put the muffin tin nearby to help them on their way. If you have an airing cupboard then you can also leave the tin in there with the door open.

CINNAMON & HAZELNUT SWIRL RYE BREAD

I'm beginning to experiment more and more with rye flour. I only use a little bit in this recipe – a 100 per cent rye loaf can be scrumptious, but also super dense and therefore not the best consistency for this enriched loaf. For me there is only one way to serve this recipe: warm, with lashings of butter that melts as it sits on top of the bread. Even the thought of the sheer indulgence is putting a smile on my face!

oil, for spraying

60g butter

120ml semi-skimmed or almond milk

300g strong white flour

120g wholemeal rye flour

I tsp sea salt flakes

7g sachet fast-action dried yeast

I tbsp honey or maple syrup (optional)

2 eggs plus I beaten egg, for glazing

For the filling

3 tbsp soft light brown sugar

2 tsp ground cinnamon

70g butter, softened

80g toasted skinned hazelnuts, finely chopped

Equipment

1.75kg loaf tin

stand mixer (optional)

Spray the loaf tin with oil and set aside.

Melt the butter in a small pan or in the microwave and then take it off the heat, add the milk and set aside.

Mix the flours, salt and yeast in a large bowl using a wooden spoon, and then make a well in the centre of the bowl and add the honey or maple syrup, if using, along with the melted butter and milk mix and two of the eggs. Mix this together to form a soft, but quite sticky ball of dough.

Place the dough onto a lightly floured work surface and knead until smooth. This should take about 10 minutes by hand and 5 minutes in a stand mixer fitted with a dough hook attachment.

To check that the dough has been kneaded enough, pick the dough up and then fold the outer edges of it underneath to make a ball with a nice taut top. Then cover your finger with flour and prod the side of the dough, making an indent, about 1cm deep – the dough should spring back all the way if it has been kneaded enough. This shows that the gluten in the dough has been worked enough and is nice and stretchy and ready for the next stage. If it is not quite ready, knead the dough for a few more minutes.

Roll out the dough on the work surface into a rectangle that is about 18 x 45cm in size, making sure that the width is no wider than the longest side of the loaf tin. If the dough keeps springing back on you, just leave it for a few moments so that the gluten can relax and it will become easier to roll.

Once the dough is rolled out to the correct size you can prepare the filling. Mix the sugar in a small bowl with the cinnamon and set aside. Spread the butter all over the dough, right out to the edges, and then sprinkle over an even layer of the sugar mixture followed by the hazelnuts.

>

CINNAMON & HAZELNUT SWIRL RYE BREAD

With the shorter side facing you, carefully roll the dough up and away from you to form a large taut sausage shape, about 18 x 10cm in size.

Tuck either end of the loaf under a little bit and then place the loaf seam-side down into the prepared tin. Spray the top with a little oil and then cover the loaf with cling film, making sure it is airtight, but that there is still plenty of room for the bread to rise. Leave the dough in a warm place for about an hour.

To check that the bread has risen enough, simply prod the side with a floured finger, as before – the bread should spring back halfway, meaning that it is ready to bake.

Preheat the oven to 200°C (fan 180°C/350°F/gas 6) and make sure the shelf in the middle of the oven is at the ready. Brush the top of the loaf with the beaten egg and bake in the oven for 15 minutes.

Reduce the heat to 180°C (fan 160°C/350°F/gas 4) and bake for another 20–25 minutes, or until the loaf is well risen and golden brown. To check that the loaf is cooked, tip it out of the tin and knock on the bottom – it should sound hollow.

Remove the cinnamon and hazelnut swirl bread from the oven and leave to cool ... Or get impatient like I do, and slice it up while it is still warm and spread thickly with butter!

If you only have a bag of strong white flour in the cupboard, you can make the loaf with that instead of using rye – it's equally as tasty! Simply use 420g of the strong white flour in the dough.

FIG & ROSEMARY RYE SODA BREAD

I am slightly obsessed by soda bread. I like the flavour a lot, but what I really love is its versatility – you can change the ingredients to give it a completely new character. I am using some rye flour here, which is an unusual addition to soda bread. It produces a slightly more dense loaf and the flavour pairs so well with the rosemary, honey and figs. Oats or a dusting of flour can top off this loaf, but brushing it with honey gives it a sticky sweet crust.

If you're making your own buttermilk, put the milk and lemon juice in a jug and allow it to sit for 20 minutes.

Preheat the oven to 200°C (fan 180°C/400°F/gas 6) and place a baking sheet in the oven. Put the plain and rye flours into a large bowl with the rosemary, salt, bicarbonate of soda and figs, and mix together with a wooden spoon. Make a well in the centre and add the olive oil or butter, honey and buttermilk, and then mix this together to form a soft dough.

Remove the baking sheet from the oven and sprinkle some flour over it. Then get your hands into the bowl and bring the dough together with a couple of turns. Turn the dough out onto a lightly floured work surface and, using your hands, form the dough into a ball with a nice taut top, tucking the edges of the ball underneath so it looks smooth on top. Flatten the ball a little bit with your hand and then pop the soda bread onto the heated baking sheet.

Being careful of the hot baking sheet, dip your wooden spoon into the bag of flour, and place it horizontally on the bread, pushing all the way down to the baking sheet to form the first half of the traditional cross which you see on soda bread. Change the direction of the spoon so it is at right angles to the other line and repeat this process to create a big cross.

Bake the bread in the oven for 30–40 minutes, or until the bread is evenly golden and crusty. To check that the bread is properly cooked, tap the base – it should sound hollow. The dough inside the cross should also be cooked and no longer wet. If the bread is not quite ready then place it back into the oven for another 5 minutes or so. Once the bread is cooked, remove it from the oven and brush it lightly with honey while the bread is still warm.

Leave the soda bread to cool a little before serving. This type of bread does not keep for too long and so it is best eaten on the day it is cooked.

340ml buttermilk or 340ml whole milk and juice of ½ lemon

425g plain flour, plus extra for dusting

75g wholemeal rye flour

1 heaped tbsp fresh rosemary, finely chopped (leaves of 3 sprigs)

1 tsp salt

1 tsp bicarbonate of soda

60g dried figs, finely chopped

40ml extra-virgin olive oil or melted butter

1 tbsp honey, plus extra to glaze

JALAPENO & PEA CORNBREAD

This is another American import that I absolutely love. I like carbs to fuel my fitness and training: heavy, dense and full of flavour. If jalapenos are tricky to find, then just use regular chillies in their place. You could use polenta instead, but choose a medium-milled variety, and if you don't have peas you can use sweetcorn or vice versa. Before you begin, it's worth drying all the veggies on kitchen paper to prevent them from leaking moisture into the cornbread.

Preheat the oven to 200°C (fan 180°C/400°F/gas 6) and grease the tin, pan or skillet. Place all of the ingredients in a bowl and mix together to form a wet batter.

Tip the batter into the prepared tin, pan or skillet and sprinkle some extra jalapenos on top. Bake for 25–35 minutes, or until a skewer inserted into the centre of the cornbread comes out clean.

Once the bread is cooked, remove it from the oven and leave it to cool a little in the tin, before cutting it into squares and serving.

200g cornmeal

100g plain or spelt flour

2 tsp bicarbonate of soda

½ tsp salt

¼ tsp freshly ground black pepper

1 egg

400ml whole milk

25g butter, melted, plus extra to grease

70g sweetcorn (tinned or frozen and thawed)

50g frozen peas, thawed

1 tbsp jalapenos, chopped, plus extra for the top (I use the ones in a jar, drained)

Equipment

20cm round springform tin or 1.2 litre ovenproof frying pan or skillet

PARMESAN, POPPY SEED & PAPRIKA STRAWS

There are two types of cheese straws – there are those made of rolled out puff pastry that is sprinkled with grated cheese, cut up into sticks and then shoved into the oven, and those that are rich, buttery and just melt in the mouth. This recipe is for the latter variety, to which I have added poppy seeds and paprika, but you can make these your own by adding flavourings such as thyme, rosemary, black pepper or dried chilli flakes.

Preheat the oven to 180°C (fan 160°C/350°F/gas 4) and line two baking sheets with baking parchment. Put all of the ingredients into a food processor and blitz for only about 20 seconds. Then tip the mixture out onto a lightly floured work surface and squidge it all together in a ball. Wrap the ball in cling film and pop it into the fridge for 20 minutes to firm up – so simple!

When the pastry has firmed up a little, sprinkle some flour on a work surface and then roll it out to a 20cm square, with the thickness of two £1 coins (about 6mm). I use a large palette knife to get it into a neat square shape. Then using a ruler, cut the dough into thirty-two long straws, each about 6mm in width. Place each one onto the baking sheets as you go. Any dough trimmings can also be baked off and kept as a cook's treat.

If the dough becomes too soft, then just put it back in the fridge for 10 minutes, or until it is easier to work with. When the straws are ready, bake them for 8–10 minutes, or until the straws are a light golden brown colour.

Once the straws are cooked, remove them from the oven, leave to cool and serve – they may seem a little soft but they will firm up. They are also super tasty when they are still warm.

100g wholemeal flour, plus extra for dusting

140g mature Cheddar cheese, grated

20g freshly grated Parmesan cheese

60g butter, softened

3 tbsp poppy seeds

1 tbsp paprika (less if you don't want them super red)

1 tbsp cold water

QUICK SUN-DRIED TOMATO, SAGE & ONION BREAD ROLLS

I used to have a bread machine, but I only used it once before giving it to a friend, because for me the beauty of homemade bread is in the making of it, and the satisfaction I draw from seeing the ingredients transformed into a big pillowy loaf. For those of you who shy away from making bread by hand for fear of it being time-consuming, these rolls may change your mind: quick homemade bread at its best.

400ml buttermilk or 400ml whole milk with juice of ½ lemon

450g self-raising flour, plus extra for rolling out and dredging

I tsp bicarbonate of soda

½ tsp salt

¼ tsp freshly ground black pepper

5 fresh sage leaves, finely chopped

5 spring onions, finely chopped

small handful of sun-dried tomatoes, well drained and blotted on kitchen towel and then finely chopped

beaten egg or whole milk, to glaze (optional)

Equipment

6cm rectangular, round or oval cutter (optional)

If you're making your own buttermilk, put the milk and lemon juice in a jug and allow it to sit for 20 minutes.

Preheat the oven to 240°C (fan 220°C/450°F/gas 8). Place the flour, bicarbonate of soda, salt and pepper into a bowl, and stir in the sage, spring onions and sun-dried tomatoes. Make a well in the centre and then pour in all the buttermilk at once. Using one hand with your fingers stiff and almost outstretched like a claw, stir in a full circular movement from the centre to the outside of the bowl. The aim is to handle the dough as little as possible to give you a softish dough that's not too wet and sticky.

When the dough has come together, turn it out onto a floured surface and gently flatten the dough with your hands or a rolling pin until it is about 2.5cm thick. Sprinkle a baking sheet with a little flour. Using a knife or cutter, cut out sixteen rolls from the dough and place them onto the dusted baking sheet as you go.

Brush the rolls with egg wash or milk if you fancy a shiny glazed look and then bake for 12–15 minutes, or until each roll is well risen, sounds hollow when knocked underneath and is a golden-brown colour. As the rolls do not contain yeast they are known as 'quick breads', and are best eaten warm on the day they are baked.

FRESH FRUIT GALETTE WITH MATCHA CREAM & BASIL

I drink matcha every morning – it gives me a great start to the day as it contains loads of good stuff as well as a little caffeine. You can leave it out of the recipe if you prefer and just use regular whipped cream, however I love its subtle flavour and colour. I always go for the Japanese ceremonial-grade matcha, which is affordable online. If you want to use non-ceremonial grade that's fine, but avoid versions labelled as 'cooking' green tea.

To make the pastry, put the flour into the bowl of a food processor along with the butter and pulse it a few times until it resembles fine breadcrumbs. Add the oats, egg yolks and salt, and a little of the water. Pulse it all together until the pastry just comes together. If you don't have a food processor, put the mixture into a bowl and rub it together with your fingertips until the mixture resembles fine breadcrumbs, then add the oats, egg yolks, salt and just enough of the water into the bowl, mixing well with a round-bladed knife.

Tip the dough onto your work surface and squidge it until it forms a ball. Wrap the ball in cling film, squish it down and pop it into the fridge for 30 minutes.

Preheat the oven to 180°C (fan 160°C/350°F/gas 4) and line a large baking sheet with baking parchment. Sprinkle a little flour on the work surface and roll out the chilled pastry to a circle, about 35cm in diameter. Use a knife to trim off odd-shaped bits to make it as round as possible.

Place the circle onto the large baking sheet, then take a little of the pastry and fold a small piece as if you were folding the corner of a page. Keep doing this until you have gone all the way around. Then prick the base all over with a fork so that the pastry does not puff up as it bakes, and brush the border and the base with the beaten egg yolk to glaze. Place the galette in the oven and cook for 25–30 minutes, or until the pastry is cooked through and is a golden brown. Once cooked, remove it from the oven and leave to completely cool down, then transfer the pastry galette to a serving plate or wooden board.

As the pastry is cooking, prepare the fruit. I like to cut up the dragon fruit to berry-sized pieces. Put the cream, icing sugar, matcha powder and vanilla into a large bowl and whisk it using a hand-held electric whisk until it reaches soft peaks but is still shiny and soft. Fill the pastry centre with the matcha cream and then pile the fruit on top. Sift a little icing sugar over the fresh fruit and then scatter over the basil or mint leaves, if you fancy it. Serve.

190g plain flour, plus extra for dusting

120g butter, cold and cut into cubes

60g porridge oats

2 egg yolks

pinch of salt

2–3 tbsp cold water

beaten egg yolk, to glaze

For the matcha cream

300ml double cream

3 tbsp icing sugar (sifted if lumpy)

2 tsp ceremonial-grade or good-quality matcha green tea powder

seeds of 1 vanilla pod or 2 tsp vanilla extract

For the fruit topping

600g prepared fresh fruit such as dragon fruit, raspberries, blueberries and grapes

icing sugar, for dusting

a few basil or mint leaves (optional)

Equipment

food processor (optional)

hand-held electric whisk

SIMPLE TREACLE TART

I was tempted to add different flavourings to this, but settled on keeping true to the treacle tart's divinely simple form. I have a huge crush on treacle tart – I can't have it in the house because if I have one slice, it soon turns into two slices and before I know it I've eaten half of the tart in a nostalgic frenzy! They served it at school and it was one of the best desserts they dished out.

Line the tart tin with baking parchment. To make the pastry, put the flour, sugar and butter in a food processor and blitz until the mixture resembles breadcrumbs. Add the egg, blitz again until the mixture comes together and then tip the pastry onto the work surface. Squidge it into a ball, wrap it up in cling film and squish it down into a thick disc. Place the dough into the fridge for about 30 minutes to rest and firm up.

When the dough has relaxed and chilled, take it out of the fridge. On a lightly floured surface, roll out the pastry to a circle, about 33cm in diameter and 5mm thick. Lay the rolling pin across the pastry and fold half of the pastry over it and then use the rolling pin to lift the pastry up over the tart tin.

Gently ease the pastry into the tin, making sure to get it into the 'corners'. I like to take a small ball of pastry, dip it into flour and then use it to gently ease the pastry into the tin. Be really careful not to stretch or pull the pastry, as this will cause it to shrink in the oven. Another tip is to dip the handle of a wooden spoon into the flour and then use it to very gently push the pastry into the 'corners' of the tin.

When you have lined the tin, trim off the excess pastry and place the tin in the fridge to firm up again for 30 minutes to relax the gluten. Preheat the oven to 180°C (fan 160°C/350°F/gas 4).

It is important to chill the pastry dough before you roll it out so that the mixture of proteins (gluten) in the dough can relax, making it easier to roll. This also makes sure that the pastry does not shrink as it cooks.

250g plain flour, plus extra for dusting

30g icing sugar

110g unsalted butter, cold and cut into cubes

1 egg

1 egg white

For the filling

80g unsalted butter

600ml golden syrup

150g brown bread, crusts removed, blitzed to fine breadcrumbs (about 4 slices, to give 100g crumbs)

2 eggs

60ml double cream

pinch of salt

Equipment

23cm loose-bottomed fluted tart tin, about 3cm deep

food processor

ceramic baking beans or dried pulses or rice

>

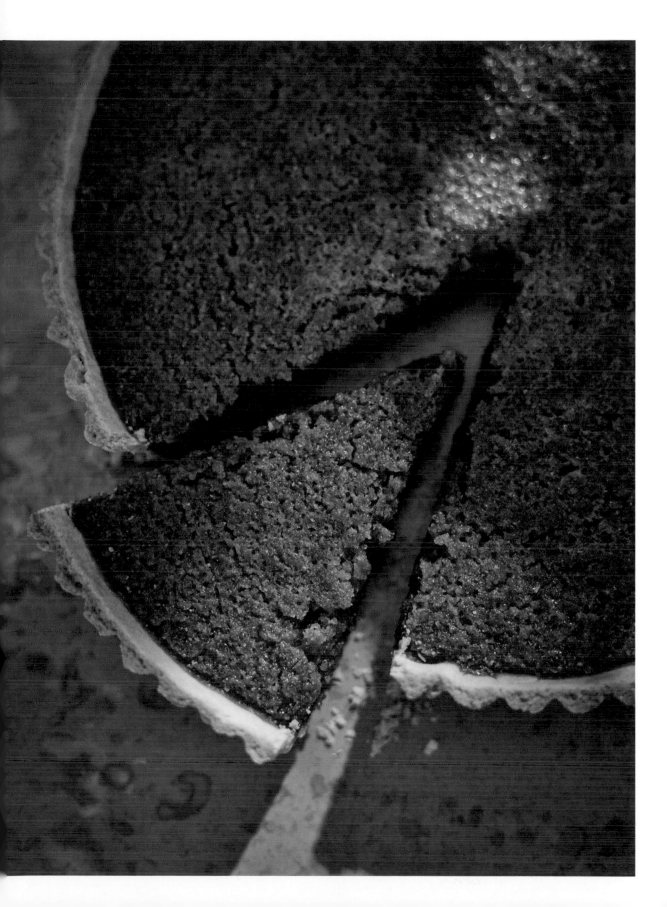

SIMPLE TREACLE TART

When the pastry is firm, remove it from the fridge. Take a piece of baking parchment and cut it into a circle, about 35cm in diameter. Scrunch it up so that it will sit in the tin, and then open it out and place it on top of the pastry case. Fill the tart tin with ceramic baking beans, dried pulses or rice, making sure they come right up the sides.

Place the tin onto a baking sheet (this makes it easier to move the tin around) and bake in the oven for 20 minutes. Then carefully draw up the edges of the parchment and remove from the pastry and discard. Brush the base with the egg white to help to seal it and avoid a soggy bottom, and then return the tart tin to the oven and bake for another 10–15 minutes, until the pastry case is golden brown and feels sandy to the touch.

While the pastry case is in the oven, make the filling. Put the butter and golden syrup into a pan and cook until melted. Remove the pan from the heat and stir in the breadcrumbs. Once this is nicely combined, whisk in the eggs, cream and salt.

Pour the filling mixture into the pastry case and then return it to the oven to bake for 15 minutes. Then turn the oven down to 150°C (fan 130°C/300°F/ gas 2) and bake for another 30 minutes, or until the tart is just set through to the centre. Once the tart is cooked, remove it from the oven and leave it to cool down.

This tart is delicious served with double cream or a good vanilla ice cream and, in my opinion, it tastes best cold.

If you think that the pastry crust is going too dark in the oven, carefully cover the crust with tin foil and then place it back into the oven to finish its baking time.

KEY LIME MERINGUE PIE WITH GINGER SNAPS

I first tried this pie in Florida, home of the famous limes. I was doing a bikini-modelling shoot with a bunch of girls. We had travelled from New York in a cramped but fun car journey. On the shoot we were given the most beautiful bright green pie for dessert. It looked so rich, creamy and fresh. I thought I would have just one bite. One bite became two large slices – it was delicious, although I had to hold in my tummy for the entire shoot!

60g butter

250g ginger snap biscuits

2 tbsp soft light brown sugar

I egg white

I quantity Swiss meringue (see recipe page 264)

For the filling

4 egg yolks

397g tin condensed milk

170ml lime juice (from about 5 standard limes, or 14 Key limes)

I tbsp lime zest, plus a little extra for decoration (optional)

Equipment

food processor (optional)

23cm loose-bottomed fluted (or straight-sided) tart tin, about 3cm deep

piping bag with 1.5cm plain nozzle

kitchen blowtorch (optional)

To make the biscuit crust, melt the butter in a small pan or in the microwave and leave to cool a little. Put the biscuits and sugar into a food processor and blitz to fine crumbs. You can also do this by hand – simply put the biscuits and sugar in a plastic bag and bash with the end of a rolling pin.

Put the crushed biscuit mixture into a bowl and stir in the melted butter and egg white until evenly combined. Tip the mixture into the tart tin and press down to make an even crust on the bottom and up the sides of the tin. Press down really, really hard so that the mixture is compact and does not crumble too much when you come to cut the pie into slices.

Pop the lined tin into the fridge to firm up for at least 10 minutes. Preheat the oven to 160°C (fan 140°C/325°F/gas 3).

Place the biscuit crust in the oven and bake for 10 minutes. When the crust is baked, remove it from the oven and set aside to cool.

Meanwhile, make the filling. Put the egg yolks into a bowl and whisk them a little, then add the condensed milk. Whisk the mixture again until everything is nicely combined. Then add the lime juice and whisk again for a couple of minutes. Taste the mixture – I like to add lime zest to give the flavour a bit more of a kick, but see whether you think it needs it or not.

Use tasty Key limes if you can find them – they are smaller and seedier than the limes we usually buy in the UK, and have a stronger scent and thinner rind.

>

Put the crust-lined tin onto a baking sheet (this makes it easier to move the tin around) and pour in the filling. Place the pie in the oven and bake for 10–15 minutes, until the filling is just set but has not changed in colour.

When the pie is baked, remove it from the oven and leave it to cool down completely in the tin. When the pie has completely cooled down, make the Swiss meringue (see page 264) for the meringue kisses. Half-fill the piping bag with the mixture – filling halfway ensures that the mixture does not squidge out of the top when you are piping.

To pipe kisses all over the pie, I usually hold the nozzle about 5mm from the surface of the filling and then squeeze the piping bag. When the meringue kiss is the size I want it to be, I stop squeezing and lift off the nozzle. Repeat with the rest of the meringue until it is all used up, making sure there are no gaps between the kisses.

The meringue has already been cooked, so simply use a blowtorch to quickly colour the kisses to a light golden brown.

When the pie is ready, serve it decorated with a little lime zest, if you fancy it. #happytummy

If you don't have a blowtorch, then pop the pie into an oven that has been preheated to 200°C (fan 180°C/400°F/gas 6) for 8–10 minutes. Keep an eye on the meringue as it can catch really quickly!

LEMON LINZER LATTICE TART

SERVES 6–8

This tart is based on the classic Austrian Linzertorte, traditionally made with jam or fresh berries. I love changing well-known recipes slightly, making them fresh to enjoy again and again. Given the chance I could eat lemon curd from the jar! Always buy the best curd you can afford or try making my recipe (page 278) as you can really taste the difference. If you want to go down the traditional route, then try a seedless raspberry jam.

To make the pastry, put the flour and almonds into the food processor with the butter and pulse until the mixture resembles breadcrumbs. Add one of the egg yolks, caster sugar, salt and cream and pulse the mixture again, just until it all comes together in a lump. You can also do this by hand by rubbing in the flour, almonds and butter between your thumb and fingers until the mixture resembles breadcrumbs, and then stirring in the egg yolk, sugar, salt and cream until the mixture just starts to come together.

Tip the dough out onto a lightly floured surface and bring it together with your hands to form a ball. Wrap the ball in cling film, flatten it a little bit and pop it into the fridge for 30 minutes to firm up, and for the mixture of stretchy proteins (gluten) in the dough to relax.

Once the pastry has firmed up a little, remove it from the fridge and cut off two-thirds of the pastry. You will use this to line the tin. Cover the remaining third with cling film and put it back into the fridge.

Lightly flour the work surface and then roll out the remaining pastry to a rectangle that is a little bigger than the flan tin, about 14 x 40cm. You want the pastry to be slightly thinner than a £1 coin (3mm). Keep the pastry moving, making sure there is always a little flour underneath it so that it doesn't stick to the surface.

Once you have rolled out the dough, use it to line the tin. Gently ease it down into the edges of the tin. I like to use a small ball of pastry covered in some flour to ease the pastry down into the corners of the tin.

The easiest way to move dough around is by using a rolling pin. Place the rolling pin across the centre of the dough, and fold one half of it over the rolling pin. Lift up the rolling pin and place it over your tin, then unfold it.

125g plain flour, plus extra for dusting

60g ground almonds

90g butter, cold and cut into cubes

2 large egg yolks

1½ tbsp caster sugar

pinch of salt

2 tsp single cream

500g good-quality lemon curd (or use recipe page 278)

To decorate
2 tbsp flaked almonds

icing sugar, for dusting (optional)

Equipment
food processor (optional)

10 x 34cm rectangular loose-bottomed flan tin, about 2.5cm deep

>

LEMON LINZER LATTICE TART

Be really gentle with the pastry, because if it is stretched at all then it may shrink or 'sink' in the tin while it cooks in the oven – it will still taste good, but it will not be super even. I like to dip the end of a wooden spoon in flour and then use this to very gently ease and press the pastry around the edges of the tin. Spend some time lining the tin if you can, as this really does make a difference once the tart is cooked.

Using a sharp knife, trim off excess pastry that is overlapping the top of the tin. Place the lined tin into the fridge for 20 minutes to rest and firm up and help stop the pastry from shrinking too much in the oven as it cooks.

Meanwhile, take the remaining third of the pastry and roll it out on a lightly floured surface into a big rectangle that is slightly thinner than a £1 coin (3mm). Cut it into long strips that are about 1cm wide. Carefully transfer these to a large baking sheet lined with baking parchment and pop into the fridge as well.

Once the pastry has firmed up nicely in the flan tin, remove it from the fridge and tip the lemon curd into it, spreading it out into a nice even layer with a spatula. Then take the pastry strips from the fridge and lay them onto the tart in a lattice pattern as shown in the picture, carefully trimming off the excess with a sharp knife or scissors. Feel free to create your own pattern if you like! Place the filled tart back into the fridge for 20 minutes to firm up and prevent the pastry from getting too soft.

Preheat the oven to 180°C (fan 160°C/350°F/gas 4) and get the centre shelf at the ready. Remove the tart from the fridge and carefully brush the top with the remaining egg yolk to glaze it and then sprinkle over the flaked almonds.

Pop the tart onto a baking sheet (this makes it easier to move the tin around) and bake for 35–45 minutes, or until the pastry is cooked through and golden brown. I like to check the tart after 25 minutes to see if it is going too dark – if it is then just cover it with a piece of foil to prevent it from going any darker.

Once the tart is cooked, remove it from the oven and leave to cool down. This is really good served both warm and cold. Dust with icing sugar, if you fancy it, then cut into slices to serve.

If you find the pastry dough is going soft and becomes difficult to handle at any point in the recipe, then simply pop it into the fridge for 5–10 minutes to firm up a little.

SALTED CARAMEL CUSTARD TART

I recently went out with two friends to a restaurant called Trinity in Clapham, London. The food was delicious, but what really stood out was their salted caramel custard tart. On the night, I endeavoured to recreate it for the home baker – and here's my version!

180g plain flour, plus extra for dusting

small pinch of salt

110g butter, cold and cut into cubes

1 egg, separated

4–6 tsp cold water

For the salted caramel custard filling

250g granulated sugar

280ml double cream

⅓ tsp sea salt flakes (I normally use Maldon)

seeds of ½ vanilla pod or ½ tsp vanilla extract

150ml whole milk

5 egg yolks

Equipment

food processor

20cm loose-bottomed fluted tart tin, about 3cm deep

ceramic baking beans or dried pulses or rice

To make the pastry, put the flour, salt and butter together in a food processor and blitz into breadcrumbs. Be really careful not to over-process it otherwise the butter will go too soft. Tip this mixture into a bowl and make a well in the centre and add the egg yolk. Mixing with a round-bladed knife, add enough of the water so that it mixes together quickly, making sure that all of the dry bits are in the dough. Then put your hands in and bring it all together. Squeeze it nice and tightly together, flatten it a little and then wrap it in cling film. Pop it into the fridge for 30 minutes to allow the mixture of stretchy proteins (gluten) in the flour to relax – this will make it easier for you to roll out the pastry.

Preheat the oven to 180°C (fan 160°C/350°F/gas 4). Get your pastry out of the fridge and roll it out on a lightly floured surface to a circle, at least 26cm in diameter, with the thickness of half a £1 coin (about 1.5mm). Place the rolling pin in the centre of the pastry and fold one half of the pastry over the top, and then lift the rolling pin and place the pastry over the tart tin. Allow the pastry to gently fall into the tin. Take a little ball of excess pastry, dip it in flour and use this to gently ease the pastry into the 'corners'. Another tip is to dip the handle of a wooden spoon into the flour and then use it to very gently push the pastry into the flutes of the tin. Be really careful not to stretch or pull the pastry as this will cause it to shrink in the oven.

When the tart is nicely lined, place the tin on a baking sheet, then take a very sharp knife and trim off the excess pastry. Then pop it back into the fridge to rest for 10–15 minutes for the pastry to firm up a little.

Be really gentle with the pastry, because if it is stretched at all then it may shrink or 'sink' in the tin while it cooks in the oven – it will still taste great, but it will not be even in size.

SALTED CARAMEL CUSTARD TART

When the pastry is firm, remove it from the fridge. Take a piece of baking parchment and cut it into a circle, about 35cm in diameter. Scrunch it up so that it will sit in the tin, and then open it out and place it on top of the pastry case. Fill the tart tin with ceramic baking beans, dried pulses or rice, making sure they come right up the sides. Place the tin onto a baking sheet (this makes it easier to move the tin around) and bake in the oven for 15–20 minutes, until the pastry looks a little set but not coloured.

Carefully draw up the edges of the parchment to remove the beans from the pastry and discard. Brush the base with the egg white to help to seal it and avoid a soggy bottom, and then return the pastry case to the oven for another 5–7 minutes, or until the base is firm and the pastry feels sandy to the touch. Take the tart tin out of the oven and set it aside, and then lower the oven temperature to 150°C (fan 130°C/300°F/gas 2).

While the pastry case is in the oven, make the salted caramel custard filling. Put the sugar into a wide-bottomed heavy-based pan and place over a medium heat. Allow the sugar to melt – don't stir it, just move the pan around every few seconds. This takes around 10 minutes, so just keep swirling the pan around now and again. The sugar will eventually turn a dark honeycomb colour, but don't allow it to get too dark as it may taste a little bitter.

When all of the sugar has dissolved, carefully add the double cream – make sure you stand back as you add it, as it will spit. Then, using a wooden spoon, stir the mixture continuously. It will go hard and look pretty dodgy but lower the heat and keep stirring it and the sugar will eventually dissolve into the cream. Once all the sugar has dissolved, add the sea salt flakes, vanilla and the milk and mix again. Take this off the heat and leave it to cool down a little.

Put the yolks in a bowl and add about one-fifth of the warm cream mixture and mix to combine with a wooden spoon. Keep adding one-fifth of the cream mixture at a time, stirring after each addition until you have added all the mixture and it is well combined. Set this salted caramel custard aside.

Pour the salted caramel custard filling into the pastry case and very carefully place it into the lower part of the oven. Bake the tart for about 45–50 minutes, or until the caramel is just set but still has a slight wobble in the centre. Once the tart is cooked, remove it from the oven and leave it to cool down completely. To serve, cut into slices with a very sharp knife. I think this is best served on its own.

BOURBON, MAPLE & PECAN TART

I often taste pecan pies when I am a judge on a US food show. I love the addition of bourbon whiskey to a regular pecan pie as it gives it a really big kick. You can of course leave this out if you are giving it to people who don't drink alcohol or to kiddies. Unlike so many American pie crusts, I don't include shortening in my pastry recipe, because I find that butter gives it a richer taste.

To make the pastry, put the flour into a food processor with the butter and blitz until the mixture resembles fine breadcrumbs. Then add the egg yolks and salt and blitz again until the dough forms a ball. If the mixture still looks a bit dry then add the ice-cold water, but add 2 tablespoons at the very most – you want a soft dough that is not sticky. If you are doing this by hand then just add the egg yolks and then, using a knife, stir the mixture until it comes together, adding the water if necessary.

Tip the dough out onto a lightly floured surface and bring the pastry together with your hands by squidging it together into a ball. Wrap the ball in cling film, flatten it a little bit and pop it into the fridge for at least 30 minutes to firm up. This helps the mixture of stretchy proteins (gluten) in the pastry to relax, making it easier to roll out the pastry. It also stops the pastry from shrinking in the oven.

Preheat the oven to 180°C (fan 160°C/350°F/gas 4). Once the pastry has rested in the fridge, use it to line the flan tin. Roll out the pastry on a lightly floured surface to a shape that is a little bigger than the flan tin, about 14 x 40cm in size and slightly thinner than a £1 coin (3mm). Put the rolling pin in the centre of the pastry and fold half of the pastry over it, then lift up the rolling pin and transfer the pastry to the tin.

Take a little ball of excess pastry, dip it in flour and use this to gently ease the pastry into the corners. Another tip is to dip the handle of a wooden spoon in the flour and use it to very gently push the pastry into the tin. Spend some time lining the tin if you can, as this really does make a difference once the tart is cooked.

> Excess liquid will help the pastry dough to come together, but it also makes the pastry slightly tough, so use as little liquid as possible.

250g plain flour, plus extra for dusting

125g butter, cold and cut into cubes

2 egg yolks

big pinch of salt

1–2 tbsp ice-cold water

For the filling

175g pecan nuts

3 eggs

90g butter

100g soft dark brown sugar

100g golden syrup

50g maple syrup

¼ tsp sea salt flakes

2 tbsp bourbon whiskey

seeds of ½ vanilla pod or 1 tsp vanilla extract

Equipment

food processor (optional)

10 x 34cm rectangular loose-bottomed flan tin, about 2.5cm deep

ceramic baking beans or dried pulses or rice

Be really gentle with the pastry, because if it is stretched at all then it may shrink or 'sink' in the tin while it cooks in the oven – it will still taste great, but it will not be even in size.

Once you have lined the tin, pop it back into the fridge for 15 minutes to let the gluten relax a little more.

Meanwhile, sprinkle the pecan nuts on a baking sheet and bake for 8–10 minutes, or until they are just beginning to colour and are lightly toasted. Keep an eye on them as they can catch and burn very quickly. Once cooked, remove from the oven and set aside 100g of the most perfect whole ones to use for decoration. Roughly chop the remaining 75g to use in the filling.

Once the pastry has relaxed for a second time, remove it from the fridge and using a very sharp small knife, cut off the excess pastry. Cut a piece of baking parchment into a circle, about 35cm in diameter. Scrunch it up so that it will sit in the tin, then open it up and use it to line the pastry. Fill it with ceramic baking beans, dried pulses or rice, making sure that they come right up the sides. Place the tart on a baking sheet (this makes it easier to move the tin around) and bake for 15 minutes, until the pastry looks set but not coloured.

Carefully remove the beans and baking parchment. Separate one of the eggs and set aside the yolk. Then brush the base of the pastry with the egg white to form a seal for the filling. Pop the pastry case back in to the oven for another 5 minutes, or until the base is firm and the pastry feels sandy to the touch, and then take it out of the oven and set it aside.

As the pastry cooks, make the filling. Put the butter, sugar, golden syrup, maple syrup and salt together in a pan over a medium–high heat, bring it just to the boil and then turn down the heat and let it simmer for 3–5 minutes over a very low heat. Remove from the heat and stir in the bourbon whiskey and vanilla and then leave it to cool down to body temperature. Add the eggs and reserved egg yolk one at a time, whisking well between each addition, and then fold in the roughly chopped toasted pecan nuts.

Pour the filling over the top to fill the pastry base. Arrange the 100g of whole pecan nuts into a lovely pattern on top.

Place the tart back on the baking sheet and bake in the oven for 15–20 minutes, or until the mixture is set but still has a little wobble to it.

Once baked, remove the tart from the oven and leave to cool slightly. Serve warm with ice cream or crème Chantilly (see page 263).

BERRY, MERINGUE & HONEYCOMB LEMON TART

SERVES 9

My whole ethos has always been to keep things simple when it comes to baking, and to cut acceptable corners without scrimping on quality. However, there are some recipes that have no corners to cut and so you just have to go all out. There are quite a few elements to this show-stopping tart, but set aside some hours in a day (or 2 days if you want to make the meringue kisses ahead of time) and enjoy the process of creating something super special.

First, make the Swiss meringue kisses. Preheat the oven to 110°C (fan 90°C/225°F/ gas ¼). Fill a medium pan with 5cm of water and place it on the hob. Bring the water to the boil over a high heat, and as soon as it is boiling, reduce to a simmer. Meanwhile, put the egg whites and sugar in a heatproof bowl and whisk them up until they become light and frothy.

Put the bowl over the now simmering water and keep whisking for 10 minutes, or until the temperature reaches 70°C (160°F) on the sugar thermometer. Once it has reached the correct temperature, remove it from the heat and pour the meringue into the bowl of a stand mixer.

Whisk the meringue on high for 5 minutes, or until the mixture has cooled down to body temperature, increased in volume and is glossy with stiff peaks. To check that the meringue is ready, pick up some of it with the whisk, then turn the whisk meringue-covered end up – the meringue should be super stiff and not floppy.

Add the plain nozzle to the piping bag and half-fill it with the meringue – filling halfway ensures that the meringue does not squidge out of the top when you are piping. Line a baking sheet with baking parchment and use some of the meringue in each corner to stick it down. The meringue will act like glue, stopping your parchment from flying around in the oven. Pipe out about 55 meringue kisses, each about 3cm in diameter, refilling the piping bag when you run out. Place the kisses in the oven to bake for about 1½ hours or until the meringues are dried out. Once the kisses are baked, remove them from the oven and leave to cool completely.

> Some say you should test the meringue mixture has been whisked enough by holding the bowl over your head – if none comes out then it is ready!

>

Ingredients

250g plain flour, plus extra for dusting

125g unsalted butter, cold and cut into cubes

2 egg yolks

2 tbsp icing sugar

large pinch of salt

1–4 tsp cream or whole milk, if needed

400g mixed berries

For the Swiss meringue

3 egg whites

100g caster sugar

For the lemon cream

500ml whole milk

zest of 4 lemons

6 egg yolks

160g caster sugar

40g cornflour

seeds of 1 vanilla pod or 2 tsp vanilla extract

For the honeycomb

40g unsalted butter, plus extra for greasing

80g caster sugar

40g golden syrup

1 tsp bicarbonate of soda

BERRY, MERINGUE & HONEYCOMB LEMON TART

As the meringue kisses are baking, make the pastry. Put the flour and butter in a food processor and blitz until the mixture resembles fine breadcrumbs. If you're using your hands, rub the butter and flour together until the mixture resembles fine breadcrumbs. Add the egg yolks, icing sugar and salt and stir them together with a knife.

Using your hands, squidge the mixture together into a ball. If the pastry feels very dry, add the cream or milk, but try to get by without it for a more tender pastry. Wrap the dough in cling film, press it down into a disc and then pop it into the fridge for 30 minutes to rest and firm up.

Roll the pastry out between two large sheets of baking parchment to a 28cm square. Carefully lift the pastry onto the rolling pin and lay it into the tin, pressing it well into the corners.

Trim the edges with a sharp knife and place the lined tin on a baking sheet. Pop the whole thing in the fridge to rest and firm again for about 15 minutes. I like to reserve pastry trimmings to patch up any cracks in the pastry as it cooks.

As the pastry is firming up, make the lemon cream. Pour the milk into a large pan, add the lemon zest and slowly bring to the boil over a low heat.

Meanwhile, place the egg yolks, caster sugar, cornflour and vanilla in a large bowl and whisk them together to combine. Just before the milk comes to the boil, remove it from the heat. Slowly pour it into the egg mixture, whisking all the time. When all of the milk has been mixed in, pour the mixture back into the pan. Cook the mixture over a medium–low heat, whisking all the time, until it thickens enough to reach 'dropping consistency'. To check that the pastry cream mixture is ready, lift up a spoonful and shake it lightly – it should fall off the spoon. Be careful not to allow the mixture to boil or overheat or the eggs will scramble.

Remove the pan from the heat and press a piece of baking parchment down onto the surface to prevent a skin from forming, then leave to cool. Pop the whole thing in the fridge until ready to use. This can be made up to a day in advance.

Preheat the oven to 180°C (fan 160°C/350°F/gas 4). Line the pastry case with baking parchment, fill with ceramic baking beans, dried pulses or rice and bake for 20 minutes. Remove the parchment and beans and return to the oven to bake for a further 10 minutes, until crisp and golden. Remove from the oven and leave to cool.

Equipment

food processor (optional)

sugar thermometer

stand mixer

piping bag with 1cm plain nozzle

23cm fluted square tart tin, about 3cm deep, or 26cm loose-bottomed fluted tart tin

ceramic baking beans or dried pulses or rice

Meanwhile, make the honeycomb. Grease a roasting tray with butter and line it with parchment paper, leaving excess hanging over the edges to lift out the honeycomb once it is set. Put the butter, caster sugar and golden syrup in a medium heavy-based pan and heat gently until the sugar has dissolved. Turn up the heat and boil rapidly, without stirring. If using a gas hob, make sure the flame doesn't 'lick' up the sides of the pan, as the sugar will start to burn here.

If some sugar does 'catch' at any point, dip a pastry brush into water and brush the sides of the pan to remove the sugar. Keep an eye on it the whole time. If the mixture goes darker on one side of the mix, then gently swirl the pan to mix it all together.

Keep boiling until the mixture goes a good golden honeycomb colour – this will take 3–5 minutes. Add the bicarbonate of soda and stir it for a few seconds to mix it in thoroughly. The mixture will foam up, so working quickly and carefully, tip the honeycomb into the lined roasting tray and leave until cold and set. Then cut or break into pieces to serve.

Fill the pastry case with the pastry cream, spreading it out evenly, and then arrange the berries on top, pointed ends facing upwards. Decorate the tart with about one-third of the meringue kisses and honeycomb pieces. Serve.

You will have leftover meringue kisses and pieces of honeycomb, as it's tricky to make smaller quantities. However, these are perfect for decorating other recipes. You can keep the kisses and honeycomb pieces between layers of baking parchment in an airtight container for up to 5 days.

CHOCOLATE MERINGUE MOUSSE TART WITH SABLE PASTRY

SERVES 8–10

The delicious tartness of lemon meringue pie makes my mouth water, but a chocolate meringue pie is a close second favourite. This is a show-stopping tart that will attract lots of attention. I have made so many meringues in my time but only recently experimented with chocolate meringue. When making mousse I prefer to use a probe thermometer rather than an old-school sugar thermometer – they are so accurate, easy and quick.

Preheat the oven to 110°C (fan 80°C/225°F/gas ¼).

Put the egg whites into the bowl of a stand mixer and whisk them until they form soft–medium peaks. Then, gradually add the caster sugar, a quarter at a time, making sure that it is well whisked before adding the next bit. Keep whisking to give shiny and stiff peaks and then set this aside. Some people say to hold the bowl over your head – if it doesn't fall out, it's ready!

Put the cocoa powder and icing sugar together in a bowl and use a balloon whisk to combine, getting rid of any lumps. Then tip this into the meringue and quickly fold together until smooth and uniform. Half-fill the piping bag with the mixture – filling halfway ensures that the mixture does not squidge out of the top when you are piping.

Line a baking sheet with baking parchment and use a blob of meringue in each corner to stick it down. Pipe thirty meringue kisses on the sheet, each about 2–3cm in diameter, then bake for about 45 minutes, or until the meringues have dried out. Once they are cooked, remove from the oven and leave to cool.

Meanwhile, make the pastry. Put the butter and the icing sugar together in a stand mixer and cream together well using a paddle attachment. Then add the egg yolk and beat until combined, making sure you scrape the bowl occasionally. Add the flour and salt, mixing just so that the mixture is uniform. You do not want to over-mix your mixture or it will become very tough. The mixture will look more spreadable than usual pastry dough, but should come together when mixed. Once well mixed, scrape the dough out of the bowl, shape it into a ball and press it down a little to form a large, thick disc. Wrap well in cling film and pop in the fridge for a good hour (or more if you can), to allow the dough to firm up and for the gluten to relax.

>

Ingredients

80g egg whites (from about 2–3 eggs)

65g caster sugar

15g cocoa powder, plus extra for dusting (optional)

65g icing sugar

For the sable pastry
120g unsalted butter, softened

50g icing sugar

1 egg yolk

160g plain flour

large pinch of salt

For the mousse
350g dark chocolate

120g caster sugar

3 tbsp water

200g eggs (about 4 eggs)

200ml whipping cream

Equipment
stand mixer

piping bag with a 1cm plain nozzle

23cm straight-sided tart tin, about 3cm deep

ceramic baking beans or dried pulses or rice

sugar thermometer

CHOCOLATE MERINGUE MOUSSE TART
WITH SABLE PASTRY

When the pastry is firm, roll it on a lightly floured surface to a circle, about 33cm in diameter, with the thickness of half a £1 coin (about 1.5mm). Use this to line the tin, making sure to get it into the 'corners'. I like to take a small ball of pastry, dip it in flour and then use this to gently ease the pastry into the tin. Try not to stretch the pastry as this may cause it to shrink. Use a sharp knife to cleanly cut the excess pastry from the edges. Pop the pastry case into the freezer for 10 minutes and preheat the oven to 180°C (fan 160°C/350°F/gas 4).

Cut a piece of baking parchment into a circle, about 35cm in diameter. Scrunch it up so that it will sit in the tin, and then open it out and place it on top of the pastry case. Fill the tin with baking beans, dried pulses or rice, making sure that they come right up the sides. Place the tin on a baking sheet and bake in the oven for 20 minutes, until lightly golden.

Meanwhile, make the mousse. Melt the chocolate in the microwave using 30-second blasts, stirring well between each blast so that it does not burn, then set this aside to cool. Put the sugar into a small pan with the water and bring it to the boil, stirring until dissolved. Pop the thermometer in and continue to boil until the mixture reaches 121°C (252°F). Meanwhile, put the eggs into the bowl of a stand mixer. As the sugar nears 121°C (252°F), start mixing the eggs until they are thick and frothy. As soon as the sugar reaches 121°C (252°F), gradually add it to the eggs while beating on top speed, making sure that the solution does not touch the whisk attachment. Once all the sugar solution has been added, beat for about 10 minutes, until the mixture has cooled, is light and fluffy and has doubled in volume. Set aside.

When the tart case has been baking for 20 minutes, take it out and carefully remove the parchment and the baking beans, then return to the oven for another 10–15 minutes for the base to cook through. Take a look after 8 minutes to make sure that the pastry does not burn. You want it to be golden in colour. Once the case is cooked, remove it from the oven and leave it to cool for 5 minutes, then put it in the fridge to cool down completely.

Whisk the cream in a medium bowl until thick and just holding its shape, being careful not to over-whisk it. Pour the melted chocolate into the whisked egg white mixture and fold to combine, very gently so that you don't knock all of the air out of it. Fold in the whipped cream until totally uniform, and set aside.

Once the pastry is cool, fill it with the mousse and pop it into the fridge for about 30 minutes to set a little. Then arrange the meringues on top, sprinkle with cocoa powder if you fancy it, and serve.

LEEK, THYME & COURGETTE TART WITH SESAME–SPELT PASTRY

My mum was a real hippy, and way ahead of her time. I grew up with lots of vegetarian food, and I know my mum would have loved this tart. When I was 15, I was a veggie for a year, but then I had a bite of someone's burger and that was it! It helps to have a mandolin to slice the courgettes in this recipe, but a sharp knife also works. If you don't want to make your own pastry then shop-bought is fine – go for a 500g packet of ready-made wholemeal pastry.

210g wholemeal spelt flour, plus extra for dusting

100g butter, cold and cut into cubes

pinch of salt

1 egg yolk

1 tbsp sesame seeds

1–2 tbsp cold water

1 egg white

For the filling

1 tbsp light olive oil, plus extra for drizzling

1 leek, finely diced

2 garlic cloves, finely chopped

1 tbsp fresh thyme leaves

200ml double cream

220g crème fraiche

4 eggs, lightly beaten

50g freshly grated Parmesan cheese

1 courgette, thinly sliced into coins (this is best done on a mandolin)

sea salt and freshly ground black pepper

To make the pastry, put the flour and butter in a food processor with the salt and blitz together until the mixture resembles breadcrumbs. Then add the egg yolk and pulse again until the dough starts to come together. Add the sesame seeds, and pulse, adding just enough water so that the mixture comes together to make a soft but not sticky dough, with no dry bits.

Tip the dough onto the work surface and bring it together to form a ball. Wrap the ball in cling film, squish it down a bit and then pop it into the fridge for 30 minutes, so that the mixture of proteins (gluten) in the dough can relax. This helps to ensure that the pastry will not shrink when it is cooked.

After 30 minutes, sprinkle a little flour on the work surface and roll out the pastry to the thickness of half a £1 coin (about 1.5mm). Then put the rolling pin across the centre of the dough and fold half of the dough over the rolling pin. Lift the rolling pin and dough up and place it over the tart tin. Carefully ease the pastry into the tart tin. Be really careful not to stretch or pull the pastry in any way, because if you do the pastry might shrink while it is cooked.

I like to use a little ball of pastry rolled up and dipped into flour to ease the pastry into the 'corners' of the tin. Take a sharp knife and trim off the excess, and then take a wooden spoon and use this to very, very gently press the pastry into the 'flutes' of the tin. Pop the tin into the fridge for 10 minutes to allow the pastry to rest for a second time.

Preheat the oven to 180°C (fan 160°C/350°F/gas 4). Cut a sheet of baking parchment into a circle, about 35cm in diameter. Scrunch it up so that it will sit in the tin, then open it up and use it to line the pastry. Fill the tin with ceramic baking beans, dried pulses or rice, making sure that they go right up to the sides of the tin. Place the tin on a baking sheet (this makes it easier to move the tin around) and place it in the oven.

>

LEEK, THYME & COURGETTE TART WITH SESAME & SPELT PASTRY

Bake the tart for 15–20 minutes, until the pastry looks like it is just beginning to set but is not coloured. Remove the tart from the oven.

Carefully draw up the edges of the parchment to remove it from the pastry and discard. Brush the base with the egg white to help to seal it and avoid a soggy bottom and then return to the oven for 5–7 minutes, or until the base feels sandy to the touch and the sides are turning a light golden brown. Once the pastry is baked, remove it from the oven and set aside. Turn the oven down to 150°C (fan 130°C/300°F/gas 2).

While the pastry is baking, prepare the filling. Heat the oil in a frying pan over a medium heat and cook the leek for 8–10 minutes, until softened but not coloured, stirring occasionally. Add the garlic and the thyme and cook for another minute, then tip this into a large jug. Add the double cream, crème fraiche, eggs and Parmesan and beat together to just combine. Season with salt and pepper.

Carefully pour the egg mixture into the cooked pastry case and then arrange a layer of the sliced courgette on top. Season the courgette slices lightly with salt and pepper and then drizzle them with a little olive oil. Return the tart to the oven and cook for another 30–40 minutes, or until the tart is cooked through but still wobbles very slightly in the centre. Remove the tart from the oven and leave to cool for a few minutes before cutting into slices to serve. This is delicious served both hot and cold.

Equipment

food processor

25cm loose-bottomed fluted tart tin, about 2.5cm deep

ceramic baking beans or dried pulses or rice

PISSALADIERE

This is a red onion, olive and anchovy tart. I have seen this with puff pastry as a base and a pizza-dough base, and far prefer the puff pastry variety – thankfully it makes it easier to whip up as well! This tart is laden with anchovies – their saltiness offsets the sweet red onions and slightly bitter olives. Lower-fat pastry does work well, but avoid the ready-rolled variety if you can as it is usually rolled too thin, and is pretty fiddly to use.

Preheat the oven to 200°C (fan 180°C/400°F/gas 6). Put the red onions in a pan with the butter over a very low heat and cook for 20–30 minutes, or until they are super soft, stirring regularly so that the onions do not catch on the bottom.

While the onions are cooking, roll out the puff pastry on a floured surface to a 36 x 26cm rectangle, slightly thinner than a £1 coin (2mm).

Using a knife, mark a border around the pastry, about 2cm wide, and then score all the way around the border in a criss-cross pattern. Without touching the border, prick the main part of the pastry with a fork. This will stop the pastry from puffing up too much as it cooks.

Place the puff pastry in the fridge to firm up a little – it is important to do this so that when it is in the oven, the flour cooks before the butter can melt into a gooey mess. When the onions are super soft, add the herbs and cook for another minute and then remove the onion mixture from the heat and leave to cool a little.

Take the pastry from the fridge and then tip the onions onto the pastry, avoiding the border. Spread them out into an even layer. Arrange the anchovies on top in a criss-cross pattern, and place an olive in the middle of each diamond shape. Season the tart with black pepper and brush the border of the pastry with the beaten egg or milk. Bake for 20–25 minutes, or until the pastry is nice and puffed up around the outside and is golden brown. Remove the pissaladière from the oven and leave to cool a little. This is great served hot or cold.

4 large red onions, finely sliced

15g butter

375g packet of puff pastry, thawed if frozen

plain flour, for dusting

½ tbsp fresh marjoram or oregano or thyme, finely chopped

2 x 50g tins anchovies, drained

60g pitted black olives

freshly ground black pepper

beaten egg or whole milk, to glaze

extra-virgin olive oil, to drizzle (optional)

It takes a little time to cook the onions down, but the tart is best when the onions are super soft.

CAKES

BANANA LOAF WITH PEANUT BUTTER FROSTING

The bananas need to be super ripe for this cake recipe. If your bananas are under-ripe, here is a neat trick to help. Simply heat your oven to 200°C (fan 180°C/400°F/gas 6) and place the bananas (in their skins) on a baking sheet. Bake them for about 15–20 minutes, or until the skins have turned black. Allow to cool a little, then peel back the banana skin to reveal soft, squishy and slightly sweet bananas. Now, will it be one slice or two?

Preheat the oven to 180°C (fan 160°C/350°F/gas 4) and line the loaf tin with baking parchment. I usually put a strip along the whole length of the tin, making sure that it comes well over the edges. This makes it easy to remove the loaf when it is cooked.

Using a stand mixer or hand-held electric whisk, cream the butter and the sugar together in a large bowl until light and fluffy. Then add one of the eggs and half of the flour and beat well, followed by the other egg and the rest of the flour along with the baking powder. Fold in the mashed bananas and then spoon the mixture into the lined tin.

Bake the loaf for about 1 hour. If after about 25–30 minutes in the oven, the bread is browning too much on top, cover it with foil. To check that the bread is cooked, insert a skewer into the centre of the loaf – it should come out clean. When the loaf is cooked, leave it to cool completely in the tin.

Once the loaf is almost completely cooled down, mix together the butter and icing sugar in a bowl using a wooden spoon, until light and fluffy. Beat in the cream cheese until it is just combined and then finally stir in the peanut butter.

When the loaf is completely cool, remove it from the tin and place it onto a plate. Using a palette knife, spread the loaf with the peanut butter frosting and sprinkle over the peanuts to decorate, if you fancy.

150g butter, softened

150g soft light brown sugar

2 eggs (at room temperature)

150g wholemeal or regular self-raising flour

1 tsp baking powder

2 very ripe bananas, mashed

handful of lightly salted peanuts, to decorate (optional)

For the peanut butter frosting

25g unsalted butter, softened

125g icing sugar

60g cream cheese

50g crunchy peanut butter

Equipment

1.2 litre loaf tin

hand-held electric whisk or stand mixer

POPPY SEED POUND CAKE

When I started out as a model in New York, at first I struggled to keep my weight down. I was so used to eating what I wanted, when I wanted, that it was an adjustment to learn that I had to eat more healthily. I did fairly well and kept my sweet treats to a minimum, but my Achilles heel was a yellow, shrink-wrapped slice of pound cake that you could find next to pretty much every shop till. The cake was so rich, dense and buttery.

Preheat the oven to 180°C (fan 160°C/350°F/gas 4) and line the loaf tin with baking parchment. I usually put a strip along the whole length of the tin, making sure that it comes well over the edges. This makes it easy to remove the loaf when it is cooked.

Put the butter and sugar in a bowl and cream everything together in a stand mixer until it is light and fluffy. You could also use a hand-held electric whisk or wooden spoon for this. Add two of the eggs and half of the flour and beat well, then add the remaining eggs and flour along with the poppy seeds and vanilla. Mix well until everything is combined.

Spoon the mixture into the lined loaf tin and then pop it into the oven for 50–55 minutes, or until golden brown and a skewer inserted into the centre of the cake comes out clean.

When the cake is cooked, remove it from the oven and leave it to cool in the tin, then cut into slices and serve.

200g butter, softened

200g caster sugar

4 eggs

200g self-raising flour

4 tbsp poppy seeds

seeds of ½ vanilla pod or I tsp vanilla extract

Equipment

1.2 litre loaf tin

stand mixer or hand-held electric whisk (optional)

I've added poppy seeds here to give the cake extra crunch, but if you want a basic pound cake (which usually has equal amounts of sugar, butter, flour and eggs) then just leave them out altogether.

CARAMELIZED BANANA & PECAN NUT BREAD

Bananas do not make much of an appearance in my house because they are a trigger for my daughter's mighty cluster headaches. However, I felt compelled to write this recipe because bananas can be simply divine when they are nestled in the warmth of bread. So my challenge was this – how can I perfect perfection? After trial and error, I found that caramelizing the bananas first is the answer.

75g butter, melted and cooled

100g soft light brown sugar

I egg

I tsp baking powder

pinch of bicarbonate of soda

200g plain flour

pinch of salt

50g pecan nuts, chopped

handful of porridge oats, to decorate (optional)

For the caramelized bananas

I tbsp hot water

2 tbsp soft light brown sugar

I tbsp butter, softened

3 large bananas, cut into thick pennies

Equipment
1.2 litre loaf tin

Preheat the oven to 180°C (fan 160°C/350°F/gas 4) and line the loaf tin with baking parchment. I usually put a strip along the whole length of the tin, making sure that it comes well over the edges. This makes it easy to remove the loaf when it is cooked.

To caramelize the bananas, put the hot water and sugar in a pan over a medium heat and then cook it for a few minutes until it just starts to go slightly darker in colour than normal honeycomb, but not super dark. Then add the softened butter and cook, stirring all the time. Add the bananas to the pan and allow them to sit in the caramel and take on a nice colour underneath as they caramelize. Flip them over then and cook them on the other side. When they have caramelized, remove them from the heat and tip them into a bowl. Mash them up with a fork, then set aside to cool down a little.

To make the cake mixture, stir the melted butter into the mashed-up bananas and add the sugar, egg, baking powder, bicarbonate of soda, flour, salt and pecan nuts and gently stir everything together. Tip the mixture into your lined tin, sprinkle with the oats, if using, and then bake for 40–50 minutes or until a skewer inserted into the centre of the cake comes out clean.

When the bread is baked, remove it from the oven and leave to cool in the tin – if you can wait, that is. I have been known to prise out the loaf and start ripping off chunks immediately!

STICKY JAMAICAN GINGER CAKE

I was born in the UK, not Jamaica. I would love to give you stories of how I would sit with the family in Kingston on a balmy evening while cake baked in the oven, but it's not so. The first time I ate gingerbread was in Ladbroke Grove back in the '90s. There was a tiny restaurant on All Saints Road – basically a Jamaican lady's front room – serving the most awesome food and cakes. It's not traditional for gingerbread, but I like to use stem ginger.

250ml buttermilk or 250ml whole milk and juice of ½ lemon

225g self-raising flour

4 tsp ground ginger

good pinch of ground nutmeg

1 tsp bicarbonate of soda

115g butter, cold and cut into cubes

115g dark brown sugar

115g black treacle

115g maple syrup, plus extra 1 tbsp for brushing on top

2 x 2cm stem ginger pieces, drained and finely chopped (about 2 tbsp)

1 egg

Equipment
1.2 litre loaf tin

If you're making your own buttermilk, put the milk and lemon juice in a jug and allow it to sit for 20 minutes.

Preheat the oven to 170°C (fan 150°C/325°F/gas 3) and line the loaf tin with baking parchment. I usually put a strip along the whole length of the tin, making sure that it comes well over the edges. This makes it easy to remove the loaf when it is cooked.

Tip the flour into a large bowl and stir in the ginger, nutmeg and bicarbonate of soda. Add the butter and then rub it in with your fingertips until the mixture resembles fine breadcrumbs.

Put the sugar into a pan with the treacle, maple syrup and buttermilk and heat until the sugar has dissolved, stirring occasionally. Increase the heat and bring the mixture up to just below boiling point and then stir in the stem ginger.

Pour the sugar and buttermilk mix into the spiced flour and butter mixture and then quickly stir everything together with a wooden spoon. Break in the egg and then beat until it is just combined to form quite a thick mixture.

Pour the mixture into the lined loaf tin, using a spatula to make sure you get all of the batter out of the bowl. Bake the loaf in the oven on the middle shelf for 55 minutes–1 hour, or until a skewer inserted into the centre of the cake comes out clean.

Once the loaf is baked, remove it from the oven and brush the top with the tablespoon of maple syrup. Leave to cool completely in the tin, then cut the sticky Jamaican ginger cake into slices to serve.

The oven temperature for this recipe is lower than for most cake recipes, but this is because it bakes for a long time.

COURGETTE & LEMON DRIZZLE LOAF WITH PISTACHIO

I was given a slice of this a while back and when my friend told me what it was, I thought … courgettes in a cake, really? But when I took a bite into that beautifully moist and flavoursome crumb, I was sold. The fact that courgettes are kind of one of your 'five a day' is an added bonus! Choose the green pistachios in the shops, not the brown dry shrivelled ones. If you can't find them then just leave them out, or substitute with hazelnuts or walnuts.

Preheat the oven to 180°C (fan 160°C/350°F/gas 4). Line the loaf tin with baking parchment and spray or brush with a little oil. I usually put a strip along the whole length of the tin, making sure that it comes well over the edges. This makes it easy to remove the loaf when it is cooked.

Place the grated courgettes in a tea towel and wring out as much of the moisture as you can over the sink. This can take a few minutes but it is an important step as the loaf may become too soggy.

Melt the butter in a pan and then put it in a bowl along with the sugar. Add the courgettes to the bowl along with the lemon zest, pistachios, vanilla and eggs and mix this together until combined. Then add the flour, baking powder and salt and carefully fold this in.

Tip the mixture into the lined tin and then bake for 1 hour or until a skewer inserted in to the centre of the loaf comes out clean.

Once the loaf is baked, remove it from the oven and set aside while you make the drizzle. Mix the lemon juice and the icing sugar together. Using a fork or toothpick, gently prick the top of the loaf and then pour the drizzle all over the cake so that some soaks into the loaf and the rest forms a light glaze on top. Remove the loaf from the tin, sprinkle the remaining pistachios over the loaf and serve.

oil, for spraying or brushing

325g courgettes, grated

120g butter

180g caster sugar

zest of 2 lemons

handful of pistachios, plus extra for decoration

seeds of ½ vanilla pod or ½ tsp vanilla extract

3 eggs

280g self-raising flour

½ tsp baking powder

pinch of salt

For the drizzle

juice of 2 lemons

60g icing sugar

Equipment

1.2 litre loaf tin

When making any cake, the less you can stir it the better for a light texture – over-stirring the mixture means that the stretchy proteins (gluten) in the flour can become overworked, resulting in a denser cake.

MATCHA, LIME & VANILLA MARBLE CAKE

Some of you may remember my Crouching Tiger, Hidden Zebra cake recipe. It had the fun effect of stripes that were only visible once the cake was cut. I have tried something similar here. The best way to make the stripes is to have a fairly wet cake mixture and to layer both mixtures a blob at a time. Repeat in this fashion to get concentric circles of batter that push each other out as you go.

Preheat the oven to 170°C (fan 150°C/325°F/gas 3) and line the loaf tin with baking parchment. I usually put a strip along the whole length of the tin, making sure that it comes well over the edges, so that it makes it easy to remove the loaf when it is cooked.

Melt the butter in a small pan or in the microwave and leave to cool a little. Put the melted butter into a bowl and add the milk, sugar and eggs. Use a wooden spoon to beat everything together well. It is best not to use a hand-held electric whisk or a stand mixer for this recipe, as they can introduce too many bubbles.

Pour half of this mixture (about 375g) into another medium bowl and stir in the vanilla. Sift in 160g flour along with ½ teaspoon baking powder, mix to combine and then set this aside.

To make your matcha mixture, put the matcha green tea into a mug and mix in the warm water until smooth. Stir this and the lime zest into the first bowl of mixture, and then sift the remaining 160g flour with the rest of the baking powder on top. Mix well to combine.

Put a tablespoon of the matcha lime mixture in the middle of the lined loaf tin. Then, using a clean tablespoon, put a blob of the vanilla mixture in the middle of the matcha lime one. Repeat this, alternating between the mixtures, so you form a type of 'bulls eye' look. Each time you dollop a blob in, the whole mixture will slowly spread out. By the time you have used up both cake mixtures, the cake batter will just have reached the edges of the loaf tin.

Pop the loaf tin on a baking sheet (this makes it easier to move the tin around) and then bake in the oven for about 1 hour 10 minutes, or until a skewer inserted into the centre of the cake comes out clean. Once the loaf is baked, remove it from the oven and leave to cool completely in the tin. Serve.

250g butter

100ml whole milk

240g caster sugar

4 eggs

seeds of ½ vanilla pod or 1 tsp vanilla extract

320g self-raising flour

1 tsp baking powder

3 tbsp cooking-grade matcha green tea powder

6 tbsp warm water

zest of 2 limes

Equipment
1.75 litre loaf tin

LEMON VICTORIA SPONGE WITH VANILLA BUTTERCREAM & LEMON CURD

The first cake I ever ate was a Victoria sponge. I remember a giant slice being presented to me at the table. The slice was at eye level and I remember doorstop layers of red, white and pale yellow. The only way to eat it was to knock it over and pull it apart! I remember the jam splodges left on the plate, and being so overcome with excitement at the flavour that I picked it up and started licking it. Safe to say this didn't go down so well with my mother!

220g butter, softened

200g caster sugar

4 eggs

220g self-raising flour

seeds of ½ vanilla pod or 1 tsp vanilla extract

zest of 1 lemon

¼ tsp baking powder

7 tbsp lemon curd (shop-bought, or make the recipe on page 278)

icing sugar, for dusting

For the buttercream

90g butter, softened

180g icing sugar

seeds of ½ vanilla pod or 1 tsp vanilla extract

Equipment

2 x 20cm round loose-bottomed cake tins

hand-held electric whisk or stand mixer (optional)

Preheat the oven to 180°C (fan 160°C/350°F/gas 4) and get the centre shelf at the ready. Line the cake tins with baking parchment.

Cream together the butter and the sugar in a large bowl. I prefer to do this with a wooden spoon, pushing the mixture onto the side of the bowl until it is mixed together and then beating it hard until the mixture turns from yellow to a paler shade. You could also use a hand-held electric whisk or a stand mixer.

Add two of the eggs to the butter mixture with half of the flour and beat together until just combined. Then add the remaining eggs and the rest of the flour along with the vanilla, lemon zest and baking powder and beat like mad to get lots of air into it.

Divide the mixture between the lined cake tins and bake on the centre shelf in the oven for 25–30 minutes, or until the cakes have shrunk slightly from the sides of the tin, are springy to the touch and a skewer inserted into the centre comes out clean. If you're using an old-style gas oven, I would recommend rotating the cakes two-thirds of the way through, as this gives a more even bake. Once the cakes are baked, remove them from the oven and leave them to cool completely in the tins.

While the cakes are cooling, make the buttercream. Cream together the butter, icing sugar and vanilla in a bowl until light and fluffy. Once the cakes are cooled down completely, place one of the cake layers on a plate and spread over the buttercream. Spoon the lemon curd over the top of the buttercream and gently place the other cake layer on top. Dust with icing sugar to serve.

To make this a traditional Victoria sponge, you can simply omit the lemon zest in the sponge and replace the lemon curd with your favourite strawberry jam.

CARROT & APPLE CAKE WITH MAPLE CREAM CHEESE FROSTING

SERVES 12–20

I wasn't sure what incarnation of carrot cake to choose. Should it be a regular cake, layered with cream cheese, or perhaps some little muffins to be devoured at breakfast and lunch? I settled on a twist on traditional cream cheese frosting. You can use many different techniques to put a special 'stamp' on your frosting. Smooth frosting works well but this swirling technique is a great skill to master.

Preheat the oven to 200°C (fan 180°C/400°F/gas 6) and line the cake tins with baking parchment.

Place all the cake ingredients into a bowl and whisk it all together well in a stand mixer or with a hand-held electric whisk. Divide the mixture between the lined tins and bake for 30–35 minutes, or until the cakes are springy to the touch, smell cooked and a skewer inserted into the centre of each cake comes out clean. Once the cakes are cooked, remove them from the oven and leave them to cool in the tins.

When the cakes have completely cooled, make the maple cream cheese buttercream (see page 264). Using a palette knife, sandwich the cakes together with a good amount of the buttercream, then spread a very thin layer over the top and sides so that the whole cake is completely covered. Place the crumb-coated cake in the fridge to set for 10–15 minutes.

When the crumb-coating has set, spread the remaining buttercream all over the cake, getting it as smooth as you can with a palette knife.

To create the swirl coating, put the cake on a rotating cake stand and hold a palette knife vertically at the base of the cake, applying a little pressure. Turn the cake stand quickly and keep holding the palette knife at this angle. Gradually move the palette knife up the cake as you turn it on the rotating stand, until you reach the top edge of the cake.

To decorate the top of the cake, start at the outside edge. Holding the knife at a 45° angle, rotate the cake as you gradually move the knife into the centre of the cake. Sprinkle over the orange zest to decorate, if using, and serve.

350ml vegetable oil

6 eggs

350g soft light brown sugar

250g carrot, grated

60g Granny Smith apple, grated (about ½ apple)

350g wholemeal or regular self-raising flour

finely grated zest of 2 oranges, plus extra to decorate (optional)

1 tsp each baking powder and bicarbonate of soda

2 tsp mixed spice

1 tsp ground cinnamon

seeds of ½ vanilla pod or ½ tsp vanilla extract

1 quantity maple syrup cream cheese buttercream (see page 264)

Equipment

2 x 23cm round loose-bottomed cake tins

hand-held electric whisk or stand mixer

rotating cake stand (optional)

GINGERBREAD &
BLACK TREACLE PARKIN

I've kept a couple of my old Home Economics books from school, and still use them to this day. The majority of British pudding recipes in the books are tempting but heavy, dense and full of dried fruit. One classic Northern English pudding is parkin: a rich dense gingerbread cake made with treacle and oats. It's highly satisfying in all the right ways.

Preheat the oven to 180°C (fan 160°C/350°F/gas 4) and line the cake tin with baking parchment. I make sure there is some extra baking parchment hanging over the edges – this makes it easier to pull out the cake when it is baked.

Put the treacle and the golden syrup into a pan, then add the butter and sugar. Put the pan on a low heat and cook until the sugar has dissolved, stirring occasionally, and then set aside.

Put the oatmeal into a large bowl with the flour, baking powder and ginger, then add the treacle mixture and mix this all together with a spatula. Tip in the milk or buttermilk with the egg and mix again until evenly combined. Spoon the mixture into the lined tin and bake for 20–25 minutes, until well risen and firm to the touch, and a skewer inserted in the centre comes out clean.

Once cooked, remove the parkin from the oven and leave to cool. Cut the cooled parkin into nine or sixteen equal-sized squares and serve.

100g black treacle

150g golden syrup

180g butter

70g soft light brown sugar

85g oatmeal (or just use regular porridge oats, which have been blitzed to a fine powder)

220g self-raising flour

1 tsp baking powder

2 tbsp ground ginger

3 tbsp whole milk or buttermilk

1 egg

Equipment
20cm square loose-bottomed cake tin

I find it helpful to use electronic scales to weigh out treacle or golden syrup. To measure, put your pan on the scales, set the scales to zero and then pour, for example, 100g directly into the pan. Stop pouring just before the digital read-out says 100g, as it takes a little time for the flow to stop. Alternatively, use a warmed metal spoon to measure it out – the warmth helps the treacle or syrup to slide off the spoon more easily!

CRANBERRY UPSIDE-DOWN CAKE WITH LEMON & GINGER

Once upon a time, cranberries were only available in winter and difficult to find unless you were lucky to know a forward-thinking grocer. Thankfully, now we can get frozen cranberries all year round in many supermarkets. It is the tartness and vibrant colour of cranberries that make them an excellent candidate for this upside-down cake. Substitute with other berries, or the more traditional pineapple slices and glacé cherries, if you wish.

30g butter

55g soft light brown sugar

200g frozen cranberries, defrosted and well drained of excess liquid

For the sponge

180g butter, softened

180g dark brown sugar

3 eggs

180g plain flour

2 tsp baking powder

4 tsp ground ginger

zest of ½ lemon

seeds of ½ vanilla pod or 1 tsp vanilla extract

Equipment

20cm round loose-bottomed cake tin

Preheat the oven to 180°C (fan 160°C/350°F/gas 4) and line the cake tin with baking parchment.

To make the cranberry layer, melt the butter and light brown sugar together in a small pan set over a medium heat, until bubbling. Cook until it turns a toffee colour, stirring constantly, and then tip into the bottom of the cake tin, tilting the tin so that it forms an even layer. Tip in the cranberries and set this aside while you make the sponge.

Cream together the butter and dark brown sugar until they are really light and fluffy. Then add two of the eggs and half of the flour and beat well until just combined. Then add the remaining egg with the rest of the flour, the baking powder, ground ginger, lemon zest and vanilla and beat well to combine.

Spoon the mixture on top of the cranberries in the tin and level out the mixture with the back of a spoon. Bake for 35–40 minutes, or until a skewer inserted into the centre of the cake comes out clean, and the cake feels springy to the touch.

Once the cake is baked, remove it from the oven and leave to cool down for a moment. Then take a large flat plate and put it upside down over the top of the tin. Holding both the tin and cake plate, flip everything over. Carefully remove the cake tin and serve. This is delicious warm or cold – serve slices with crème Chantilly (see page 263) or ice cream.

CHOCOLATE ESPRESSO & ALMOND BATTENBURG CAKE

This is my play on a traditional Battenburg. For best results, buy white marzipan rather than the Day-Glo yellow version, as this gives more of a mellow colour that can match the colour of the sponge. Cakes are for sharing with friends and family, and I love this cake because it is the perfect choice for a man – it's a long way from the light and fluffy yellow and pastel pink colours of a classic Battenburg!

Preheat the oven to 180°C (fan 160°C/350°F/gas mark 4), and make sure the shelf in the middle of the oven is at the ready. Line the loaf tins with baking parchment.

Put the butter and sugar together in a bowl and, using a wooden spoon, cream them together until they are light and fluffy. Add the baking powder with half of the flour, all of the ground almonds and two of the eggs and beat it like mad for a moment. Then add the rest of the flour and the remaining egg with the milk and beat hard again. Transfer half of the cake mixture to another bowl, add the cocoa powder and coffee essence to it and then fold together to combine.

Put the plain almond cake mixture into one of the lined tins and the chocolate espresso cake mixture into the other. Smooth down the tops with the back of a spoon and bake for 20–25 minutes, or until the cakes are springy to the touch and a skewer inserted into the centre of each cake comes out clean.

Leave the cakes to cool down completely in the tins and then trim them into two equal-sized rectangles, 20 x 6cm in size and 3cm high.

Cut each rectangle lengthways down the centre to give you two identical strips of chocolate cake, and two identical strips of white cake. Set the cakes aside.

Sprinkle a little icing sugar on your work surface, and then roll out the marzipan to a large 15 x 24cm rectangle, slightly thinner than a £1 coin (about 3mm).

180g butter, softened

180g caster sugar

½ tsp baking powder

140g self-raising flour

30g ground almonds

3 eggs

3 tbsp whole milk

40g cocoa powder, plus extra for dusting (sifted if lumpy)

2 tsp Camp coffee essence

icing sugar, for dusting

250g white marzipan

120g apricot jam

Equipment
2 x 1.2 litre loaf tins

> Keep in mind that the cakes may take different times to cook because of the different ingredients in the mixtures.

>

CHOCOLATE ESPRESSO & ALMOND BATTENBURG CAKE

Warm the apricot jam in a small pan. Sandwich together a white cake strip and a chocolate cake strip with a little of the apricot jam, making sure the edges meet just right. Repeat with the other two strips so you have two blocks.

Take one of the blocks and cover it with a thin layer of apricot jam, and then place the other block on top, making sure that the dark strip is above the white strip. Have a play around for a moment making sure that everything lines up nicely.

Spread the top of the cake with apricot jam and place this side down in the centre of the marzipan. Spread the exposed marzipan with the rest of the jam and fold each side of marzipan over the cake so that its seam meets slightly in the centre at the top of the cake. Gently seal the edges together by pressing with your fingers and then flip the cake over onto a serving plate.

Take a wide palette knife and hold it lengthways along the centre of the cake. Sprinkle some icing sugar or cocoa powder over the top to decorate. Voila – the perfect cake for the man in your life!

OUT OF AFRICA GIRAFFE SWISS ROLL WITH ORANGE CREAM FILLING

I love a cake recipe with a sense of humour! This cake transforms a Swiss roll-style sponge with an animal print finish. The recipe is actually really quick to make and will look better and better every time you make it. This is a really fun one to make with the kiddies too.

5 egg whites

120g caster sugar

5 egg yolks

30g unsalted butter, melted

30ml double cream

85g plain flour

1 tsp vanilla extract

10g cocoa powder

1 scant tbsp water

For the filling

150ml double or whipping cream

2 tbsp icing sugar, sifted

seeds of ½ vanilla pod or 2 tsp vanilla extract

finely grated zest of 1 orange (or to taste)

1 tbsp Cointreau (optional)

1 tsp whole milk (optional)

Equipment

23 x 33cm Swiss roll tin

disposable piping bag

Preheat the oven to 180°C (fan 160°C/350°F/gas 4), and make sure the shelf in the middle of the oven is at the ready. Line the tin with baking parchment. I make sure there is some extra baking parchment hanging over the edges – this makes it easier to pull out the cake when it is baked.

Put the egg whites in a bowl and whisk until they reach medium peaks – they wont be super stiff, but they will be starting to hold their shape. Then add half of the sugar and whisk up until the mixture reaches super stiff peaks that are white and shiny, and then set that aside.

In another bowl add the egg yolks and the other half of the sugar and whisk until the mixture goes really light and fluffy and thickened, and then fold the two mixtures together until combined. Fold in the butter and double cream until well combined and then carefully pour one quarter of this mixture into another bowl. This will be your white mixture and the remaining three-quarters will be your chocolate mixture.

Sift 55g of the plain flour into the bowl for the white mixture and add the vanilla. Fold in gently until just combined and then spoon the mixture into a piping bag. Snip off a little of the piping bag tip to give a 1cm opening and then pipe lines all over the parchment to resemble a 'giraffe skin' pattern. Go all the way up to the edges and leave quite large holes, so that there is space for your chocolate mixture to sit. Once you have done this, pop the tin into the oven for about 5 minutes. You want the mixture to cook through but not colour. Then, remove from the oven and set aside.

Next, sift the remaining 30g of flour and the cocoa powder into the bowl for the chocolate cake mixture. Add the water, and fold in gently.

I like to add 1 scant tablespoon water to the chocolate Swiss roll mixture, as this helps to stop the sponge from cracking when you roll it up.

>

OUT OF AFRICA GIRAFFE SWISS ROLL WITH ORANGE CREAM FILLING

Pour the chocolate mixture over the cooked mixture, and level it off with a spatula or palette knife. Bake in the oven for about 10–15 minutes, or until the cake is springy to the touch and cooked all the way through.

When the cake is cooked, remove it from the oven and leave to cool for 5–10 minutes. Then peel off the baking parchment and let it cool down completely.

Meanwhile, make the filling. Whisk the cream, icing sugar and vanilla together in a bowl until the mixture is just holding itself. Add the orange zest and Cointreau, if using, and fold this together until the mixture is firm but not grainy. If it is grainy it means that it is over-whisked, so add 1 teaspoon of milk to loosen it up a little if necessary. Set the filling aside in the fridge until needed.

Once cooled, carefully turn the sponge out on a piece of baking parchment, pattern side-down. Spread the sponge with the whipped orange cream, going right up to the edges.

With a short side facing you, roll up the edge really tightly using the baking parchment to help. Make sure that you tuck the first roll in nice and tightly as this will give the roulade a well-defined swirl. Continue to roll up the rest of the Swiss roll carefully and evenly and then place it seam-side down on a piece of cling film, and wrap it up tightly like a sausage.

Put the wrapped Swiss roll in the fridge for 15 minutes to set, then remove it from the fridge, unwrap and serve.

CHOCOLATE, PEAR & HAZELNUT BROWNIE CAKE

This cake is best served gooey in the middle and ever so slightly under-cooked. It is part cake, part brownie and part fondant – basically all of my favourite chocolate desserts rolled into one!

Preheat the oven to 180°C (fan 160°C/350°F/gas 4) and line the baking tin with baking parchment. Melt the butter in a small pan over a low heat or in the microwave. Remove the butter from the heat and add the chocolate. Leave to sit for a couple of minutes and then stir very briefly until smooth. Set aside.

Put the eggs and the yolk into the bowl of a stand mixer, and using the whisk attachment, whisk it until it is really light, fluffy and mousse-like, or reaches the ribbon stage. To check that it has reached the right stage, lift up some of the mixture on the whisk and let it fall back down – it should sit on the surface of the mixture for 6–8 seconds before slowly disappearing back in. You can also use a large bowl and a hand-held electric whisk or a balloon whisk, but it might take a little time.

When it has reached the right consistency, add the soft light brown sugar and whisk until the mixture is light and mousse-like. To check that the mixture is ready, pick up a little mousse with the whisk and then let it drop back into the mixture. It should sit on the mixture for 6 seconds before it sinks.

Add the flour to the egg and sugar mixture with the salt and gently whisk this all together. Fold in the melted chocolate mixture and the hazelnuts, using as few stirs as possible to keep the air in. Make sure you mix in all of the flour and hazelnuts. Then tip the mixture into the lined tin, pouring from a low height so it does not knock all of the air out of it.

Arrange the pear slices on top of the cake mixture and bake in the oven for 20–25 minutes, or until it is just cooked but still has some gooeyness in the middle – expect it to have a bit of a wobble.

When the cake is ready, remove it from the oven and sprinkle with the extra toasted hazelnuts and then leave to cool a little before serving. Serve warm or cold, sprinkled with icing sugar if you fancy it.

150g butter

150g dark chocolate (preferably 70% cocoa solids), roughly chopped

3 eggs

1 egg yolk

100g soft light brown sugar

80g self-raising flour

pinch of salt

160g toasted skinned hazelnuts, finely chopped, plus a handful extra to decorate

2 firm ripe pears, cored and thinly sliced

icing sugar, for dusting (optional)

Equipment

20cm square cake tin

stand mixer or hand-held electric whisk (optional)

RAINBOW ROULADE WITH LIME CREAM CHEESE CHANTILLY

It is good to have a repertoire of cake recipes for anniversaries and birthdays. This one is great for kids, but it also works for adults, especially if you tailor the cake to their favourite colours. There are many different types of food colouring to use – gel, fondant and liquid colouring. I like to use the gel or fondant ones as you need to use a lot of the liquid variety to get strong colours, and this can adjust the consistency of the mixture.

5 egg whites

120g caster sugar

5 egg yolks

30g unsalted butter, melted, plus extra for greasing

30ml double cream

60g plain flour

selection of gel or fondant food colourings such as red, yellow, orange, purple and green

For the lime crème Chantilly

150ml double or whipping cream

150g full fat cream cheese

2 tbsp icing sugar

seeds of ½ vanilla pod or ½ tsp vanilla extract

zest of 1–2 limes (to taste)

Equipment

23 x 33cm Swiss roll tin

5 x disposable piping bags

Preheat the oven to 180°C (fan 160°C/350°F/gas 4) and make sure the shelf in the middle of the oven is at the ready. Grease the Swiss roll tin and line it with baking parchment.

Put the egg whites in a bowl and whisk them until they reach medium peaks – they won't be super stiff, but they will be starting to hold their shape. Then add half of the sugar and whisk until the mixture comes to super stiff peaks that are white and shiny, and then set aside.

In another bowl, whisk the egg yolks and the rest of the sugar until the mixture goes really light, fluffy and thickened. Fold the two mixtures together until combined. Then fold in the melted butter and double cream until well combined, sift over the plain flour and fold in well until uniform.

Split the mixture between however many colours you want. I have chosen red, yellow, orange, purple and green. Add the gel food colouring a little at a time to each one, folding it in gently so as not to knock out too much air. Then spoon each mixture into a separate piping bag and snip the tip of each one to give a 1cm opening.

Place the tin so that the shorter side is in front of you. Starting in the top right-hand corner of the tray, pipe a line of each colour, running diagonally across to the opposite bottom left-hand corner. The lines will run diagonally across the tin. When all the colours have been piped once, repeat until all the mixture is used up and you reach the other side of the tin. Try to repeat the order of colours. You will end up with about four lines of each colour.

I like to lay the five piping bags out in the order they are used and then replace each bag after I've piped a line, to prevent me from mixing them up.

>

RAINBOW ROULADE WITH LIME CREAM CHEESE CHANTILLY

Place the tray in the oven and bake for 10–15 minutes, or until the cake is cooked through and springy to the touch, and then set aside to cool.

Once the sponge is cool, make the lime crème Chantilly. Place the cream, cream cheese, icing sugar, vanilla and lime zest in a bowl and mix together with a wooden spoon or spatula until smooth and thick but spreadable.

Put a chopping board over the top of the sponge and flip it over. Peel off the baking parchment and then trim the rectangle so it is even with squared-off edges. Spread the cream over the sponge in an even layer, spreading right up to the edges.

With a short side facing you, roll up the edge really tightly. Make sure that you tuck the first roll in nice and tightly as this will give the roulade a well-defined swirl. Continue to roll up the rest of the roulade carefully and evenly and then place it seam-side down on a piece of cling film, and wrap it up tightly like a sausage.

Place the wrapped roulade into the fridge to set for 30 minutes–1 hour, then remove it from the fridge, unwrap and serve.

BAKED OREO RICOTTA & CREAM CHEESE CHEESECAKE

SERVES 8–12

Strange as it might seem, I don't enjoy eating Oreos straight out of the packet – I am a milk chocolate digestive girl at heart. However, Oreos are brilliant for baking – you can crush or blitz them into breadcrumbs for cakes, brownies and cheesecakes. They are very rich, so I have given the option to use digestives for the base instead. This cheesecake is very moreish – it's really hard not to eat the whole thing in one sitting!

Preheat the oven to 160°C (fan 140°C/325°F/gas 3) and line the cake tin with baking parchment.

Put the amount of butter you need for your base recipe into a pan over a low heat and melt completely. Leave to cool, and then blitz the digestive biscuits or Oreo cookies in a food processor. Tip the biscuit mix into the pan and mix it together so that all of the crumbs are covered.

Tip the mixture into the lined tin and pack it really tightly using a palette knife or wooden spoon. I like to put all of my weight on it as I press down to get a nice even layer. Pop the base into the fridge to set.

Meanwhile, make the filling. Blitz the Oreos to small bite-sized crumbs in a food processor. Tip the biscuit crumbs into a bowl and add the cream cheese, ricotta, cream, eggs, caster sugar and cornflour and mix together until combined. Beat it just enough so that the mixture is uniform. Take the base from the fridge and pour this mixture on top, levelling it with the back of a wooden spoon.

Place the cheesecake on a baking sheet (to make it easier to move around) and bake it in the oven for 45–50 minutes, until it is just set but still has a little wobble in the centre. Then turn off the oven and leave it in there for about an hour with the door slightly ajar.

> Instead of using a food processor, you could choose to pop the biscuits into a large plastic bag and bash them with a rolling pin to get the crumbs.

>

For the biscuit base
75g butter

200g digestive biscuits (about 15)

Or for the Oreo base
25g butter

200g Oreo cookies (about 17)

For the filling
115g Oreo cookies (about 10)

500g cream cheese

150g ricotta cheese

150ml double cream

3 eggs, lightly beaten

60g caster sugar

2 tbsp cornflour

For the topping
8 Oreo cookies, broken into pieces (optional)

icing sugar, for dusting (optional)

Equipment
23cm springform cake tin

food processor

BAKED OREO RICOTTA & CREAM CHEESE CHEESECAKE

Make sure that the cheesecake has cooled down completely and then remove it from the oven.

Carefully release the cake from the tin, gently peeling the baking parchment from the sides of the cake. You can serve it as it is, or decorate with broken Oreo cookies and/or a light dusting of icing sugar.

Leaving the cheesecake to cool in the oven is the best way to avoid cracking. Don't move it while it cools, just leave it be to do its thing. If it does crack, don't worry – it will still taste delicious.

CRUST-LESS LEMON CHEESECAKE WITH VANILLA

I first came across a crust-less cheesecake in Manhattan – it's like a naked version of the Big Apple staple. Leaving the cheesecake to cool in the oven helps to stop it from cooling down too quickly and cracking down the middle. It is not a guarantee however, and if yours should crack while cooling, it will not affect the delicious flavour at all.

700g full-fat cream cheese

100g butter, softened

100g caster sugar

zest of 2 lemons

seeds of ½ vanilla pod or 1 tsp vanilla extract

3 large eggs, lightly beaten

300g crème fraiche

Equipment
23cm springform cake tin

Preheat the oven to 160°C (fan 140°C/325°F/gas 3). Half-fill a large deep roasting tin with water and place this on a baking sheet. This will be your bain-marie, so make sure your cake tin fits into the roasting tin comfortably.

Check that your tin is watertight by pouring water into it. If it leaks slightly, you can make a 'cradle' with tin foil. To do this, put a piece of tin foil on the work surface and then place the tin on top. Bring the tin foil up over the edges a bit and squeeze it all in tightly to ensure it doesn't let any water in or any cheesecake mixture out. Line the base and sides of the cake tin with baking parchment. Place the roasting tin and baking sheet into the oven.

Put the cream cheese in a large bowl with the butter, caster sugar, lemon zest and vanilla and mix together well with a wooden spoon or spatula. Add the eggs and the crème fraiche and stir so that the mixture is just combined. It is best not to overbeat the mixture at this stage, or you will end up with lots of air bubbles in your finished cheesecake. Pour this mixture into the lined tin and then carefully place it in your heated bain-marie. Cook for 40–45 minutes, or until the cheesecake is just cooked through but still has a slight wobble in the centre.

Once the cheesecake is cooked, turn the oven off and leave the cheesecake to cool down in the oven for about 90 minutes with the oven door slightly ajar. This helps to stop the cheesecake from cracking as it cools down slowly. When you are sure that it has cooled down completely, remove from the oven and then carefully release it from the tin, gently peeling the baking parchment from the sides of the cake. Slide the cheesecake onto a serving plate and serve.

The roasting tray acts as a bain-marie and prevents the cheesecake from getting too hot and over-cooking or curdling in the oven.

ZEBRA CHEESECAKE

Lots of you loved my Crouching Tiger, Hidden Zebra cake, so I thought I would apply the same technique to this cheesecake. You can use two ice-cream scoops to form the striped effect, or I find it easier to pipe the different mixtures.

Preheat the oven to 140°C (fan 120°C/275°F/gas 1) and line the base of the tin with baking parchment. Blitz the biscuits in a food processor to fine crumbs, and tip them into a bowl and add the butter. Stir together until well blended and tip into the base of the tin. Use the back of a spoon to push the biscuits down to a compact layer. I usually spend a good 3–4 minutes pushing down with my full body weight.

Melt the chocolate in a glass bowl in the microwave in 30-second blasts, stirring well between each one. Don't blast it for longer than this as you may burn the chocolate. When the chocolate is melted, set it aside to cool.

Put the cream cheese, mascarpone, icing sugar and eggs in a large bowl and beat together until smooth. Split the mixture into two batches of 600g and 375g. Add the vanilla and 1 tablespoon cornflour to the larger amount and beat in well until smooth. Blend the milk with the remaining tablespoon of cornflour until smooth. Add this to the smaller mixture along with the cooled melted chocolate and mix until well blended.

Using a spatula, spoon each mixture into a separate disposable piping bag. Snip off the end of each bag to give a 2–3cm opening. Pipe a blob of the chocolate mixture into the centre of the tin (about 2 tablespoons). Pipe about the same amount of the vanilla mixture into the centre of the chocolate blob and repeat until all of the mixture is used up. Eventually the mixture will reach the edges of the pan, creating an interesting effect. Bang the tin gently on the surface occasionally to help the mixtures to move outwards.

Sit the tin on a baking sheet (to make it easier to move around) and pop into the oven to bake for about 30–35 minutes, or until the cheesecake is cooked but still has a little bit of wobble in the centre. When the cheesecake is cooked, turn the oven off and let the cheesecake cool down completely in the oven. When the cheesecake is cool, remove it from the oven and serve.

14 digestive biscuits

100g unsalted butter, melted

For the filling

140g dark chocolate (at least 64% cocoa solids), roughly chopped

600g cream cheese

100g mascarpone

150g icing sugar, sifted

3 eggs

seeds of 1 vanilla pod or 1 tsp vanilla extract

2 tbsp cornflour

50ml whole milk

Equipment

23cm springform cake tin

food processor

2 x disposable piping bags

CHOCOLATE, COFFEE & HAZELNUT PETIT GATEAU WITH RED MIRROR GLAZE

I have had so many requests for this recipe: the ace of stunning desserts! At first I had my reservations as it requires specialist equipment and ingredients that can be expensive. However, it is show-stopping for a special occasion. You can order 8cm flexible 5-hole half-spherical moulds, gold grade gelatine and neutral glaze from catering suppliers. To cut a corner in the recipe, you can use Madeira cake instead of making the joconde sponge.

First make the joconde. Preheat the oven to 180°C (fan 160°C/350°F/gas 4) and line the Swiss roll tin. Put the icing sugar and ground hazelnuts into a bowl with the flour, salt and eggs. Beat well with the hand-held electric whisk for a good 8–10 minutes, until the mixture is light, fluffy and thickened. Then add the melted butter and beat for another minute until combined.

Put the egg whites in a separate bowl and whisk until they reach medium peaks. Then gradually add the soft light brown sugar, whisking all the time until you have a stiff and shiny meringue. You want to whisk them until they reach a stiff peak – you can do this in a stand mixer or with a hand-held electric whisk. If you do it by hand with a balloon whisk it will take some time, but it will be a great workout!

To check that the meringue is ready, take some on the end of the whisk, then turn the whisk meringue-covered end up – the meringue should be super stiff and not floppy. Some people say to hold the bowl over your head and then if it does not come out it is ready!

Tip the egg whites into the flour and nut mixture and fold together quickly to make sure everything is combined, then tip the mixture into the lined tin and spread it out so that it is even.

Place the tin in the oven and bake for 10–12 minutes, or until the sponge is cooked through, has a nice light brown colour and a skewer inserted into the centre comes out clean. Remove from the oven and set aside to cool. The sponge should be about 1cm thick.

Once the sponge has cooled down a little, use the 6cm cutter to cut out ten circles and the 3cm cutter to cut out another ten circles. Place these into the freezer to firm up. Save leftover cake for making cake pops or trifle.

>

60g icing sugar

60g toasted hazelnuts, finely ground

20g plain flour

pinch of salt

2 eggs

1 tbsp melted butter

2 egg whites

20g soft light brown sugar

For the chocolate mousse

4 leaf gelatine sheets (8g in total)

200ml whole milk

2 tsp instant coffee powder

350g double or whipping cream

250g dark chocolate (at least 70% cocoa solids), finely chopped

For the mirror glaze

240g white chocolate, finely chopped

9 gold-grade gelatine sheets (20g in total)

CHOCOLATE, COFFEE & HAZELNUT PETIT GATEAU WITH RED MIRROR GLAZE

As the sponge is firming up, make the mousse. Put the gelatine leaves in a bowl and cover with cold water. Set this aside for the gelatine to soften. Put the milk into a pan and bring it just to the boil, then as soon as it is boiling take it off the heat and stir in the instant coffee powder. Leave it for 2–3 minutes to cool down. You don't want it to cool down too much – it needs to be used at a specific temperature a couple of stages on. While this is cooling down, whisk the double or whipping cream until it just starts to thicken, but before it reaches soft peaks.

When the gelatine is very soft and squidgy, remove it from the cold water. Make sure you take all of it out – because gelatine is a clear substance, it can sometimes get lost in the bowl.

Squeeze the gelatine out, discarding as much of the water as you can, and then put the softened gelatine into the still hot milk and whisk it together until the gelatine has completely dissolved. It is good to work quickly at this stage, as the milk needs to be pretty hot when you combine it with the chocolate.

Put the dark chocolate into a bowl, add half of the milk mixture to it and whisk together to combine. Then add the rest of the milk mixture and mix well. This chocolate milk mixture needs to be 43°C (86°F). You may need to carefully heat it or cool it down a little depending on the temperature. Once it has hit the right temperature, add the whipped cream and fold it together so it is combined. Pour this mousse mixture into the moulds, making sure that it only comes about two-thirds of the way up.

Remove the sponge discs from the freezer and place the smaller ones onto the mousse. Press each disc down so that it goes almost all the way down but not through to the bottom of the sphere. Place each large disc on top of each sphere, pressing down only a tiny bit. Fill each sphere to the top with chocolate mousse and use a palette knife to scrape along the top of the spheres to level them. Place the filled moulds into the freezer for 2–3 hours to firm up or even overnight if you want to carry on making this the next day.

When the gateaux are firm, keep them in the freezer and make the mirror glaze. Put the white chocolate in a tall container (the one that comes with the stick blender is great, however a tall jug works well). Put the gold gelatine in a bowl and cover with some cold water and set aside for the moment.

> I like to use a probe or laser thermometer rather than a sugar thermometer, as I find it reads the temperature more quickly.

120ml water

240g glucose syrup (at room temperature)

240g white caster sugar

170g condensed milk

100g neutral glaze

⅛ tsp red gel food colouring (use Sugarflair for the bright colour)

To decorate

10 raspberries

edible gold leaf (optional)

Equipment

23 x 33cm Swiss roll tin, about 2.5cm deep

hand-held electric whisk or stand mixer

6cm round cutter

3cm round cutter

sugar thermometer (ideally a probe or laser thermometer)

2 x 8cm flexible 5-hole half-spherical moulds

stick blender

Put the 120ml water, 240g glucose and 240g caster sugar into a small pan over a low heat and allow the glucose to dissolve. Bring the mixture to the boil and heat until it reaches 103°C (217°F). As soon as the temperature reaches 103°C (217°F), whisk in the soaked gelatine (being sure to squeeze out all of the excess water and discard the soaking water) and then quickly pour it onto the white chocolate.

Use the stick blender to combine it all together, moving the blender slowly around the container. Make sure that you don't bring the blender above the surface of the chocolate mixture otherwise this will cause bubbles to appear – the trick is not to get any bubbles into this. Once it is smooth, add the condensed milk and the neutral glaze along with the food colouring and blend again until smooth, this should take a few minutes. Again, make sure the stick blender does not come above the surface of the liquid, as this can cause bubbles to appear. Allow the glaze to cool to 28–31°C (81–87°F) – this takes about an hour.

Once the glaze is ready to use and at the correct temperature, cover your work surface with some cling film and then put a rack on top. Depending on the size of your rack, you may need to use two racks so that the gateaux are spaced out. Remove the gateaux from the freezer and pop each one out onto the rack, flat-side down.

Pour the glaze steadily over the centre of each gateau, allowing the glaze to flow over the top and sides for a smooth coating and the excess to fall into the cling film below. If you think the covering looks thick, use a palette knife to very gently scrape the excess off the top. Give each gateau a second covering and then allow to set.

If you put them into the fridge they can lose their shine, so it is best to leave them in a cool dry place to set and then serve. However, if you have to put them in the fridge, the shine will usually come back when the cakes warm up.

Use a palette knife to loosen and lift each gateau from the wire rack. Arrange them on a serving plate, and then decorate with one of the raspberries and edible gold leaf, if desired. Serve.

If bubbles appear on the mirror glaze as it cools, then pop it into the fridge overnight and let the bubbles and foam come to the top. Once you are ready to cover the petits gateaux, scrape off the bubbles and foam and bring the temperature of the mixture back to 28–31°C (81–87°F).

PEACH, MAPLE & FIG COBBLER

This American pudding comes in sweet and savoury incarnations and its toppings vary to the extreme – some are made with cold butter like a British crumble, and others are made with melted butter that is poured over the fruit like a batter. Some are rolled out like pastry and stamped with a cookie cutter, and others still are just dolloped on top. I opted for the last variety, as I loved its buttery taste and the neat 'crazy-paving' look.

Preheat the oven to 180°C (fan 160°C/350°F/gas 4) and use the knob of butter to lightly grease the pie dish. Tip the peaches into the prepared dish with the figs, maple syrup and cinnamon, and then mix well to evenly combine. Set aside.

To make the topping, melt the butter in a small pan or in the microwave and leave to cool a little. Put the flour and sugar into a bowl and mix well with a wooden spoon. Then add the melted butter and salt and stir until the mixture starts to come together.

Take a small handful of the dough (about 50g) and squidge it together into a ball, then flatten it out a little and place on top of the fruit. Continue with the rest of the topping to make nine balls that sit side by side on top of the fruit.

Place the pie dish into the oven and cook for 40–45 minutes, or until the topping is cooked through and golden brown and the fruit is bubbling around the edges. This cobbler is best served warm with fresh cream, ice cream or custard.

knob of butter

6 firm ripe peaches, cut into wedges (stones discarded – you can peel them if you fancy but I don't)

3 firm ripe figs, cut into quarters

3 tbsp maple syrup

1 tsp ground cinnamon

For the topping

160g butter

150g plain flour

180g soft light brown sugar

pinch of salt

Equipment

1.2 litre pie dish

If you would like extra texture and crunch, scatter some chopped nuts or porridge oats on top of the cobbler just before baking it in the oven.

SALTED CARAMEL CREME BRULEE

This is a very easy dinner party dessert with a subtle creamy flavour. It takes a little patience to get just right. Prepare the crème brûlées up until just before the sugar goes on top and then, a little before you are ready to serve, blowtorch the sugar on top and away you go – you have a sugary glass top that should crack with a touch of a spoon. You can also make these in ten 150ml ramekins but you will need to adjust the cooking time accordingly.

First, make the caramel to flavour the custard. Place the sugar in a heavy-based pan with the water and heat gently, stirring only until the sugar has dissolved. Use a wet pastry brush to brush any stray bits of sugar off the side of the pan, otherwise this sugar can cause the mixture to crystallize into a hard ball.

Once the sugar has dissolved, increase the heat to medium–high and bring it to the boil. Let this bubble away vigorously, until the caramel turns quite a dark honeycomb colour. You can swirl the pan from time to time to make sure everything is turning evenly, but do not stir it at this stage, otherwise it may crystallize into a hard lump. Once the caramel has come to the right colour, remove it from the heat and carefully add 4 tablespoons of the cream, reserving the rest of the cream for later in the recipe. Add the salt, stirring the mixture slowly with a wooden spoon until evenly blended. Stir in the butter, a couple of cubes at a time, until you have achieved a smooth caramel. Set aside to cool completely.

When the salted caramel has cooled down, preheat the oven to 150°C (fan 130°C/300°F/gas 3). Lightly whisk the egg yolks in a large glass bowl and set aside. Then bring the rest of cream to the boil in a clean pan with the vanilla. Once it is boiling, remove the pan from the heat and whisk this heated cream into the bowl with the egg yolks, then add the caramel to the egg yolks and stir to combine.

Sit the glass bowl over a large pan of hot water over a low–medium heat and heat it until the mixture starts to thicken, stirring all the time with a spatula. It should change to the consistency of single cream.

Divide this mixture between the ramekins or moulds. Place them in a large roasting tin and pour warm water into the tin, making sure none goes into the ramekins. You want the water to come three-quarters up the sides of the

60g granulated sugar

1 tbsp water

1 litre double cream

1½ tsp sea salt flakes

50g butter, cut into cubes

12 egg yolks

seeds of 2 vanilla pods or 4 tsp vanilla extract

For the topping

6 tbsp granulated sugar

Equipment

8 x 200ml ramekins or moulds, 7.5cm high

kitchen blowtorch

>

SALTED CARAMEL CREME BRULEE

ramekins. This makes a bain-marie that will prevent the mixture from getting too hot and curdling in the oven.

Place the bain-marie on the middle shelf in the oven and cook for 20 minutes. To check that the crème brûlées are cooked, use an oven glove to remove one of them from the water and then shake it gently. There should still be slight movement in the centre of the custard. If it is still runny, put it back in the oven and check after another 5 minutes or so.

Remove the cooked crème brûlées from the oven and allow them to cool. Pop them into the fridge until you are ready to finish them off and serve them.

Just before you serve the brûlées, sprinkle them liberally with an even layer of the granulated sugar, making sure the top of each one is completely covered. I like to use a blowtorch for this part. Keep the blowtorch moving over the top so that the sugar does not burn and the custard underneath does not overcook. Heat the topping until it starts bubbling and turns a medium golden-brown colour.

Once you have a lovely crunchy topping on each crème brûlée, leave them to cool down completely (the sugar gets silly hot!) and then serve.

You can also caramelize the topping under the grill but it can take a long time, and the delicately cooked custard underneath can overcook.

PISTACHIO PAVLOVA WREATH WITH RASPBERRIES, LYCHEES & LIME

Let me introduce the Pavlova celebration wreath! This recipe is so pretty, easy to make and has an incredible flavour. I make this meringue in the French style – this is the easiest of all meringues and does not require a sugar thermometer. The ingredients are always the same: double the amount of sugar to the weight of the egg whites. For best results, I recommend that you weigh out the egg whites to get exactly the amount you'll need.

For the meringue
5 egg whites
250g caster sugar
50g icing sugar
2 tsp cornflour

For the raspberry sauce
200g raspberries
2 tbsp icing sugar
¾ tbsp lime juice
pinch of lime zest
2 tsp arrowroot or cornflour
I tbsp water

To decorate
400ml crème Chantilly (see page 263)
75g raw unsalted pistachio nuts, lightly toasted
200g raspberries
100g tinned lychees, well drained and cut in half
finely grated zest of 2 limes

Preheat the oven to 140°C (fan 120°C/275°F/gas 1) and make sure the shelf in the middle of the oven is at the ready.

To get really well whisked up egg whites, make sure the bowl and all the other equipment are super clean. Put the egg whites into the bowl of a stand mixer and whisk the eggs on medium speed, until they just begin to go frothy and hold their shape a little in the bowl. You can also use a hand-held electric whisk or you can even whisk it by hand using a balloon whisk, but this does take a long time.

Put the sugars together in one bowl, stirring to combine. With the speed on medium–high, add about one third of the sugar in a steady stream, whisking all the time. The mixture will now begin to thicken a little – just make sure that all of the sugar crystals have dissolved before you add the next batch. Add the next third and repeat the process again, whisking it all up really well. Then add the final third of the sugar and whisk on high – you can whisk on high now as the egg mixture will be much more stable. Keep whisking until the meringue forms stiff peaks.

Add the cornflour and fold in with a metal spoon or spatula. To check that the meringue is ready, take some on the whisk and turn it meringue-covered end up – the meringue should be super stiff and not floppy. Some people say to hold the bowl over your head – if it doesn't fall out, it's ready!

Draw a 25cm circle on a piece of baking parchment – you can do this free-hand or draw round a 24cm round cake tin. Draw a 10cm circle in the centre to create a nice even ring shape that can act as the stencil for your wreath.

This recipe uses icing sugar as well as caster sugar, because icing sugar makes the Pavlova a little chalkier and therefore gives a slightly lighter result.

PISTACHIO PAVLOVA WREATH WITH RASPBERRIES, LYCHEES & LIME

Equipment

stand mixer or hand-held electric mixer (optional)

food processor

Flip the parchment over. Put four blobs of the meringue mixture onto a baking sheet and then place your wreath stencil on top. The meringue will act like glue, stopping your parchment from flying around in the oven.

Use the spatula to place large dollops of the meringue onto the 'ring', making sure to keep it within the edges of the stencil. Make sure that the dollops are the same height – this will mean the wreath will bake more evenly and give you a pretty finish. When all of the meringue is on the stencil, I like to run a spoon around the top to smooth it out slightly as this makes it easier to put the fruit on once it has been baked.

Put the Pavlova into the oven and bake for about 55 minutes–1 hour. The meringue will get a little colour on it but not much at all. Once it is baked, remove from the oven and leave to cool. While the meringue is cooking, you can prepare the raspberry sauce.

Blitz the raspberries in a food processor with the icing sugar, lime juice and zest, and then using a spatula, scrape the raspberry mixture into a small pan. If you don't want the raspberry seeds in it, you can use a fine sieve to remove them. Mix the arrowroot or cornflour with the water, making sure there are no lumps and then add this to the raspberry mixture and stir together. Arrowroot will give you a crystal clear sauce and cornflour will be just a little cloudier. Bring the mixture to the boil over medium–high heat and then as soon as it is boiling, turn down the heat and simmer gently for a few minutes, until it has thickened, stirring occasionally. Then remove from the heat and set aside to cool.

Carefully slide your Pavlova wreath onto a large flat serving plate. If it cracks a little that is totally okay! Place dollops of the crème Chantilly around the top of the wreath, being as messy or as neat as you like. Then drizzle over some of the raspberry sauce – the rest of the sauce can be served in a jug or bowl at the table. Decorate the Pavlova wreath with the raspberries, lychees and pistachios, scatter over the lime zest and serve.

Choose brightly coloured ingredients for your decoration, such as bright green pistachios rather than brown ones. I always use tinned lychees as they look pretty, but by all means use fresh!

LEMON & THYME MACARONS

Macarons get a bit of tough rap for being hard to make, but with enough time and a good recipe everyone can master our little French sandwiched friends! If you don't fancy the combination of lemon and thyme then make the recipe without thyme, but give it a try as the pairing is delicious! I am using lemon extract in place of juice for a punch of flavour without sacrificing the macaron structure. For best results, use a water-based, gel colouring.

Draw round the reverse end of the 1cm piping nozzle to make twenty circles on two sheets of baking parchment, giving you forty circles in total. Make sure you space them out a little. Flip the parchment over and use it to line two large baking sheets.

Put the granulated sugar into a pan with the water over a medium heat. Cook gently until the sugar has dissolved and then turn the heat up and let it bubble away until the mixture reaches 118°C (244°F). I like to use a probe thermometer rather than an old-fashioned sugar thermometer. They read temperatures so much more quickly, but an old-school thermometer also works.

As this bubbles away, put the icing sugar and the ground almonds into a food processor and blitz this to a very fine powder and then set it aside.

Once the sugar mixture has reached about 108–109°C (226–229°F), start to whisk 60g egg whites (half the total amount) in a stand mixer on a low–medium speed. Once the temperature of the sugar mixture reaches 118°C (244°F), remove the pan from the heat, then turn up the stand mixer to a medium–high speed and add the sugar mixture in a steady stream, making sure that the sugar does not touch the whisk. You can also do this with a hand-held electric whisk but it will take longer. This method of making meringue is called Italian meringue, and it makes a very stable meringue that is great for macarons. Some people prefer using a cold method (French) or a warm method (Swiss) to make the meringue. I have tried all three methods and they all work, but an Italian meringue is especially good for a more solid structure.

> Baking parchment can blow around quite a bit in the oven, so once I have made the macaron mixture, I like to use a blob underneath each corner of the baking parchment to act as glue.

For the macarons
165g granulated sugar

40ml water

165g icing sugar

165g ground almonds

120g egg whites

few drops of lemon extract

1 tsp fresh thyme leaves, plus extra for decoration

few drops of yellow gel food colouring

For the lemon buttercream
85g butter, softened

zest of 1 lemon

200g icing sugar

85g cream cheese

Equipment
piping bag with a 1cm plain nozzle

sugar thermometer

food processor

stand mixer or hand-held electric whisk

pastry scraper (optional)

>

LEMON & THYME MACARONS

When you have added all of the sugar mixture to the egg whites, add the lemon extract with the thyme and turn up the speed. Then add the food colouring, bit by bit until it becomes the right colour for you. Make sure it has a slightly stronger colour than you want for your baked macarons, because when you add the icing sugar and almond mixture to the bowl at a later stage the colour will dilute somewhat. Keep mixing the Italian meringue mixture until the bowl is no longer hot and cools to body temperature. Once it reaches body temperature, set this aside.

As the meringue is whisking, mix the blitzed icing sugar and ground almonds with the remaining 60g egg whites in another bowl. Keep stirring this together and it should get quite stiff. Set this aside.

Once the meringue mixture is ready, add half to the almond mixture, mixing well until just combined. Then add another quarter of the meringue mixture and mix well until just combined before repeating with the final quarter.

Now it is time for the macaronage of the mixture. Take a pastry scaper (or a spatula) and press the mixture up against the inside of the bowl a few times, folding the mixture over as you go. Take some of the mixture and then drop it back into the bowl. This process deflates the mixture just enough to reach the right lava-like consistency – they say it takes about forty 'strokes' for the process to give you a shiny mixture that holds its shape without being too runny or leaving a pointy top.

To check that the mixture is ready, take some mixture and then drop it back into the bowl – it should sit on the surface of the mixture for about 15–20 seconds before sinking into the mixture.

When the mixture has reached the correct stage, use it to half-fill the piping bag – filling halfway ensures that the mixture does not squidge out of the top when you are piping. Pipe the mixture into the templates on the lined baking sheets. Once you have piped the macarons, bang each tray lightly on the work surface to settle them, and then allow them to rest for 10–15 minutes. Preheat the oven to 150°C (fan 130°C/300°F/gas 2).

Bake the macarons in the oven for 12–15 minutes, until crisp and firm. Once the macarons are baked, remove them from the oven and leave to cool completely, before lifting them off the baking parchment with a palette knife.

Once the macarons are completely cool, make the buttercream. Put the butter into the bowl of a stand mixer and beat it really well, then add the lemon zest and the icing sugar and beat again. If you are using a hand-held electric whisk, then add the icing sugar little by little so that the icing sugar does not fly everywhere, and mix well between additions. Add the cream cheese to the bowl, beating well until smooth. If you find that the buttercream has become too soft, then just pop it into the fridge for 10 minutes or so to firm up.

When the buttercream is ready, use it to half-fill the piping bag and pipe blobs of buttercream onto twenty of the macaron shells, making sure there is enough to come to the edges of the shell when it comes to sandwiching them together. Gently sandwich the shells together and serve. Enjoy!

You can sandwich the macarons with lemon curd as well if you fancy it. Simply omit the lemon zest from the buttercream (otherwise it will all taste too lemony) and instead of piping the buttercream over the whole surface of the shell, pipe it just around the edge, spoon lemon curd in the middle and then sandwich them together.

STRAWBERRIES & CREAM MERINGUE LAYER CAKE WITH FRESH MINT

SERVES 10–12

This is an Eton-mess type of layer cake – when you cut into it, you won't get fine slices like a cake but it will crumble into a very tasty creamy, crunchy mess. When assembled and brought to the table, wait for the 'oohs' and 'ahhs' before people dig in. This method for making meringue is known as the 'reverse method' because you add the sugar first – give it a shot and see if you prefer making it this way!

You will need to make five meringue layers for this layer cake. I have a double oven with a small top bit and a bigger bottom bit which works well for this, but if you have one oven then you may need to cook the meringue layers in batches. Preheat your oven(s) to 150°C (fan 130°C/300°F/gas 2).

Line five baking sheets with baking parchment, then draw a 23cm circle on each piece of paper and flip it over so that the markings don't make contact with the meringue. Again, if you don't have five baking sheets of a suitable size, you may need to do this in batches.

Put the granulated sugar into a large bowl and then add three of the egg whites. Whisk this up until it is really stiff and shiny. You can use a hand-held electric whisk or a stand mixer fitted with a whisk attachment if you fancy it.

Once the mixture is stiff and shiny, add another egg white, continuing to whisk the mixture until stiff. Add the rest of the egg whites like this, one at a time, making sure that the mixture is whisked up before the next addition, until you have added all of the egg whites and the mixture is super stiff and shiny. To check that it is ready, take some of the meringue on the end of the whisk, then turn the whisk meringue-covered end up – the meringue should be super stiff and not floppy.

There is a neat way and a messy way to do the next stage. For the messy way, spoon the meringue onto the marked circles, being sure to stay within the lines. For a neater version, half-fill the piping bag with the meringue – filling halfway ensures that the mixture does not squidge out of the top when you are piping. Starting on the outer edges of each circle, pipe the meringue into a spiral shape going round and round in ever-decreasing circles until you finish at the centre. Repeat with the other four circles.

>

550g granulated sugar

10 egg whites

800g strawberries

For the cream filling

600ml double cream, well chilled

seeds of 1 vanilla pod or 2 tsp vanilla extract

3–4 tbsp icing sugar (to taste, depending on how sweet you like things)

To decorate

icing sugar, for dusting

mint leaves, to decorate (optional)

Equipment

hand-held electric whisk or stand mixer (optional)

piping bag with 1cm plain nozzle (optional)

STRAWBERRIES & CREAM MERINGUE LAYER CAKE WITH FRESH MINT

Place the meringues into the oven and bake (in batches if need be) for about 1 hour, or until the meringues are crisp and cooked through. Then remove them from the oven and leave to cool completely.

Once the meringues are completely cool, make the cream filling. In a large bowl, whisk the cream, vanilla and enough of the icing sugar to taste until it is just beginning to hold. Place a small blob of the cream filling on a serving plate and then take one of the meringue layers and place it on top. This will help the cake to stick on the serving plate and not move around as you layer.

Reserving 400g of the prettiest strawberries for the top, finely slice the remaining strawberries.

Carefully spread 2 tablespoons of the cream filling on the bottom meringue with a spoon. Scatter a quarter of the chopped strawberries over the cream, then take another 2 tablespoons of the cream and spoon this over the top of the strawberries (so your next meringue layer will stick on top of it).

Repeat with three more of the layers: spreading 2 tablespoons of the cream on each layer, then a quarter of the chopped strawberries, followed by 2 more tablespoons of the cream filling. Carefully place each layer on top of the layers beneath. For the top layer, pop the final meringue circle on the top of the stack and spread with the remaining cream. Arrange the whole strawberries all over the top, then sprinkle over the icing sugar and mint leaves, if using. Serve.

If you fancy adding flavour to the cream filling, heat 200ml port in a small pan over a medium heat until it has reduced by three-quarters, then leave it to cool down completely and fold it into the whisked cream filling.

LEMON MERINGUE ECLAIRS WITH FRESH CREAM & RASPBERRIES

I've given these éclairs a twist by substituting choux pastry with Italian meringue. This kind of meringue has the same ratio of sugar to egg as Swiss meringue, but the sugar is heated to make a syrup, which is then added to the egg whites to give a more stable and strong texture. This recipe calls for lemon curd, which you can choose to buy or make from scratch (see page 278).

240g granulated sugar

100ml water

4 egg whites

For the filling

250ml double cream

60g lemon curd (see page 279 or use shop-bought)

12 raspberries

Equipment

sugar thermometer (optional)

stand mixer or hand-held electric whisk (optional)

piping bag with 1cm star nozzle

piping bag with 1cm straight nozzle

To make the meringue, put the sugar and the water into a pan over a low heat and allow the sugar to dissolve. Have a pastry brush standing in a cup of hot water nearby and use this to brush down any sugar on the sides of the pan, as this may cause the mixture to crystallize into a lump.

Once the sugar has dissolved, turn up the heat a little and let the mixture bubble away. To check that it is ready, take ½ teaspoon of the sugar syrup and drop it into a mug of cold water. Wait for 15 seconds for the sugar to harden, then pull out the sugar with your fingers – it should be a little ball that is firm to the touch. If the ball does not form, then the sugar syrup needs to be cooked for longer. You can also use a sugar thermometer to test when the sugar syrup is ready. The temperature needs to read 120°C (250°F).

When the sugar syrup is almost ready, start whisking the egg whites. Whisk them until they are almost at stiff peaks. I like to do this in my stand mixer, but you can also use a hand-held electric whisk or a balloon whisk.

As soon as the sugar syrup is ready, carefully add it to the egg whites in a steady stream, whisking all the time, making sure that the sugar syrup does not touch the whisk. Keep whisking until the meringue is stiff and shiny with a stiff peak.

Take the piping bag fitted with the star nozzle and half-fill it with meringue. Line two baking sheets with baking parchment and dab a little of the meringue under each corner of the baking parchment. The meringue will act like glue, stopping your parchment from flying around in the oven.

Pipe twelve éclair 'halves' onto a baking sheet, each 8cm long. Repeat on the other baking sheet to give you twenty-four halves in total. Place the sheets into the oven to bake for about 1 hour, or until the meringues are firm to

>

the touch, crisp and well dried out, but still white. Switch the baking sheets around halfway through baking to ensure even cooking.

Once the meringues are cooked, remove them from the oven and leave them to cool completely. Once they are cool, carefully take them off the baking parchment and place them on a plate. Whisk the cream in a bowl until soft peaks form and then take the piping bag fitted with the straight nozzle and half-fill it with the whipped cream. Filling halfway ensures that the cream does not squidge out of the top when you are piping. Set the piping bag aside.

Put twelve of the meringue halves flat-side up onto a serving plate, securing them with a little dollop of cream so that they do not fall over. Spoon 1 teaspoon of lemon curd on top of each one and pipe about 1 tablespoon of whipped cream on top of the lemon curd. Place the other meringue halve on the top to sandwich it together, and then repeat with the rest of the lemon meringue éclairs.

Decorate each lemon meringue éclair with a raspberry, gluing it on with a little dab of the remaining whipped cream, and serve.

MILLEFEUILLE WITH VANILLA CREME PATISSIERE & FEATHERED FONDANT ICING

Classic millefeuilles are also known as Napoleons. They are filled with crème pâtissière (pastry cream) and sport a white and brown feathered top, just like this one. I have also included a recipe for Red velvet Napoleons (page 186), if you want to vary the flavours and fancy trying a slightly different method of layering the pastry. Both recipes are equally striking and simple to make but – like all things worth the effort – they will take a little time.

Before you start, make sure you have three large baking sheets that can fit inside your fridge. Line each of the baking sheets with parchment paper.

Cut the pastry into three equal pieces and then lightly flour a work surface. Take one of the pieces and roll it into a rectangle, slightly larger than 14 x 36cm, with the thickness of half a £1 coin (roughly 1.5mm). Repeat with the other two pieces of puff pastry, giving you three roughly equal rectangles of pastry. Fold up any excess pastry carefully so that the lovely layers inside the pastry don't get lost, and pop it into the fridge (to use within a couple of days) or into the freezer (to use within a month).

Take one of the puff pastry rectangles and carefully transfer it onto one of the lined baking sheets. Repeat with the other pastry rectangles and lined baking sheets, and then put them all in the fridge for at least 30 minutes to firm up and allow the gluten in the pastry to relax – this prevents the pastry from shrinking in the oven.

Preheat the oven to 220°C (fan 200°C/425°F/gas 7) and prepare three shelves in your oven. As the pastry is firming up, make the crème pâtissière. Put the egg yolks and sugar into a bowl and stir together gently using a whisk – you just want to combine them rather than getting air into the mixture. Then add the cornflour, mix until combined and set aside.

Put the milk in a medium pan with the vanilla and place over a medium heat, until just boiling. As soon as it just hits the boil take it off the heat. Pour 2 tablespoons of this hot milk mixture into the egg mixture in the bowl, stirring the egg mixture all the time. Add the rest of the milk to the egg mixture, whisking to combine.

> Keep stirring the egg mixture in the bowl as you pour in the hot milk to make sure that the eggs don't scramble.

600g puff pastry (see page 271 or 3 x 320g all-butter ready-rolled packets)

a little plain flour, for dusting

For the crème pâtissière
12 egg yolks

340g caster sugar

80g cornflour

1 litre whole milk

seeds of 2 vanilla pods or 4 tsp vanilla extract

To decorate
100g pouring fondant icing (use fondant icing sugar or see recipe on page 262)

45g spreadable chocolate fondant icing (use fondant icing sugar or see recipe on page 262)

Equipment
piping bag with 1cm straight nozzle

off-set palette knife

small disposable piping bag

>

When the mixture is fully combined, pour it back into the same pan that you used to heat up the milk. Place the pan on a medium heat and cook for about 8–10 minutes, or until the mixture is bubbling and has thickened, stirring all the time to make sure the mixture does not catch on the bottom of the pan. Remove the pan from the heat and spoon the mixture into a bowl, covering it with baking parchment to stop the mixture from forming a skin on the top. Set aside to cool down completely.

Take the pastry rectangles out of the fridge, then take one baking sheet and cover it with a sheet of baking parchment, making sure that the whole of the pastry is covered. Then place an empty baking sheet or roasting tin on top of the baking parchment, to weigh the pastry down. This will stop the pastry from puffing up in the oven. Repeat with the other two baking sheets, so all three puff pastry baking sheets are weighed down. Place them in the oven and bake for 22–25 minutes. Carefully, using oven gloves, have a peek to check the pastry. It should be crisp and have gone from pale to a darkish golden brown.

Once the pastry is cooked, remove it from the oven and leave it to cool for a moment. Then, using oven gloves, carefully lift the baking sheets that are weighing the pastry down and gently peel off the baking parchment on top. Set the pastry aside to cool down for a few moments. Then slide one of the puff pastry rectangles onto a chopping board and using a large sharp serrated knife and a ruler, trim down each rectangle until it is 12 x 35cm in size. Use a pastry brush to gently brush off excess crumbs. Repeat with the other two rectangles, giving you three equal-sized rectangles.

Take the crème pâtissière and beat it well with a wooden spoon to loosen it. Half-fill the piping bag with the mixture – filling halfway ensures that the mixture does not squidge out of the top when you are piping.

Pipe the crème pâtissière all over one of the pastry rectangles. I usually start on the outside edge and then go all the way around the edge – I keep going round and round until I reach the centre of the pastry. Repeat with another pastry rectangle so you have two pastry rectangles covered with pastry cream. Put one of the covered pastry rectangles on top of the other and pop it into the fridge to set, so that the millefeuille does not collapse under its own weight.

> I like to get a little pedantic when I cut the pastry to size, and use a set square to get the corners straight! Make sure you very gently saw the knife back and forth to cut the pastry, and avoid applying pressure on the delicate pastry.

Make up both fondants according to the packet instructions or use the recipes on page 262. Make sure both fondants are spreadable but thin enough to pipe. When you're happy with the fondants, put the chocolate fondant in a small piping bag and set it aside, leaving the white fondant in the bowl.

Put the remaining pastry rectangle on a wire rack with one of the long edges facing you. Pour over enough of the white fondant to give a thin even layer, making sure you cannot see any pastry through it, then use a small off-set palette knife to quickly spread the fondant right to the edges.

Using scissors, snip off a tiny bit of the end of the chocolate fondant piping bag giving you a small hole that you can use to pipe a fine line. Pipe six fine, straight lines along the length of the pastry rectangle.

Take a toothpick or skewer and use it to gently drag down vertically through the chocolate lines. Then drag through the chocolate lines again, 2cm along from the first line, but this time move from the bottom to the top. Repeat this process, doing a line up and then a line down all the way along the pastry to make a pattern as shown in the photograph. I do about six lines in total.

Leave the fondant to set for 5 minutes, and then using a serrated knife, cut the rectangle into seven 5cm-wide strips all the way along the pastry from left to right. Wipe the edge of the knife with a damp cloth or paper towel between each cut. Arrange the pastry strips on a flat baking sheet and return them to the fridge to set.

Once the crème pâtissière is set, remove the layered pastry from the fridge. Place it in front of you with one of the long sides facing you and then, using a sharp large serrated knife, carefully cut it into seven 5cm-wide pieces. These will fit identically with the already cut and feathered fondant-iced tops. Finish each one with a feathered fondant-iced rectangle top and arrange on a serving plate. Serve and enjoy!

If the fondant icings are too thick then they won't spread properly. If they are too thin they may bleed into each other and dribble off the top of the millefeuille. By all means do a little test on a piece of baking parchment, if you like.

RED VELVET NAPOLEONS WITH REDCURRANTS & RASPBERRIES

Napoleons are stunning but relatively easy-to-make layered pastries, also known as millefeuilles. For this really show-stopping dessert, you can make all the components ahead of time and then assemble just before serving. You can fill them with all sorts of flavours and ingredients. Feel free to make these your own with a pastry cream or a fresh and easy crème Chantilly (see page 263).

Before you start, make sure you have two large baking sheets that can fit inside your fridge. Line each of the baking sheets with parchment paper.

Cut the puff pastry in half and then roll each piece out on a lightly floured surface to a rectangle slightly larger than 15 x 36cm. Use the rolling pin to lift the pastry rectangles onto the lined baking sheets. Put them in the fridge for at least 30 minutes to firm up and allow the gluten in the pastry to relax, preventing the pastry from shrinking in the oven.

Preheat the oven to 200°C (fan 180°C/400°F/gas 6). Take the pastry rectangles out of the fridge and cover each one with another sheet of baking parchment. Then lay another heavy baking sheet on top – preferably one that is the same size as the one beneath. If your tray isn't heavy, weigh it down with an empty ceramic ovenproof dish. Bake for 22–25 minutes, or until the pastry is crisp and golden brown. Carefully, using oven gloves, have a peek to check the pastry. It should have gone from pale to a strong golden colour.

Once the pastry rectangles are cooked, remove them from the oven and sprinkle with a little icing sugar. Turn the grill onto a medium heat and pop each pastry rectangle underneath for the icing sugar to melt and caramelize a little, or use a blowtorch if you have one. This process takes seconds, so keep an eye on it so it does not burn.

Remove the pastry rectangles from under the grill and leave to cool down completely. Using a very sharp knife and a ruler, trim each piece to make precise 15 x 36cm rectangles.

You will need to divide each rectangle into nine smaller rectangles, each 5 x 12cm in size. To do this, place a rectangle on the work surface so that a long side is facing you. Cut it widthways into three pieces of the same size, and then

600g puff pastry (see page 271 or use 2 x 320g all-butter ready-rolled packets)

a little plain flour, for dusting

icing sugar, for dusting

For the filling

50g good-quality white chocolate, roughly chopped

300g butter, softened

750g icing sugar

seeds of 1 vanilla pod or 2 tsp vanilla extract

few drops of red food colouring (I use Sugarflair red extra)

300g cream cheese

To decorate

icing sugar, for dusting

6 sprigs of redcurrants

175g raspberries

small handful of tiny fresh mint leaves (optional)

>

RED VELVET NAPOLEONS WITH REDCURRANTS & RASPBERRIES

cut each of the thirds into another three pieces. Repeat this process with the other large pastry rectangle until you have eighteen rectangles, each 5 x 12cm in size.

To make the filling, melt the white chocolate in a heatproof bowl set over a pan of simmering water. Make sure the base of the bowl does not touch the simmering water. You can also melt the chocolate in 30-second bursts in the microwave, stirring until melted. Leave to cool.

Put the butter and icing sugar in a stand mixer and whisk really well until light and fluffy, then add the vanilla and the cooled melted chocolate and beat for another moment. Add the red colouring, whisk again and then add the cream cheese and whisk for a moment. Don't over-whisk the cream cheese otherwise it will go runny. Once the filling is ready, use it to half-fill the piping bag with the mixture – filling halfway ensures that the mixture does not squidge out of the top when you are piping.

Take six pastry rectangles and put them on a baking sheet lined with baking parchment. Pipe equal-sized blobs of filling all the way along the border of each shape, then fill in the centre – you don't have to be super neat for the middle bit as only the outside blobs will be visible. Half-fill the piping bag again. Put the second layer of pastry on top of each piped rectangle and pipe again in the same way as you did for the bottom layer. You should now have six almost finished Napoleons.

To decorate, put a small palette knife in the centre of one of the remaining pastry rectangles – you can either do this so it is straight down the centre or at an angle. Sprinkle icing sugar all over the top, leaving an undusted stripe where the palette knife has been. Repeat with the rest of the tops and then place each one on top of the layered pastries, giving each Napoleon three tiers. Put a little blob of the filling at the end of each Napoleon to act as glue and arrange the redcurrants and raspberries on top.

Serve and enjoy. You can also garnish with some mint leaves if you fancy it.

Equipment
kitchen blowtorch (optional)
stand mixer
piping bag with a 5mm nozzle

If the filling gets too runny, that's fine – simply pop it into the fridge to firm up a little. For a deeper red colour, add some more colouring and beat well until evenly combined.

COFFEE ECLAIRS WITH ESPRESSO & TOASTED HAZELNUT CREAM

There is a little shop in South Kensington that sells perfect éclairs that are beautiful. The shop looks more like a jewellery shop than a patisserie one! Inspired by these I decided on this simple yet delectable éclair, perfect for an afternoon tea. Bread flour is 'thirstier' than regular flour, so if you use a mixture in choux pastry you can add more eggs, which give the éclairs a lovely rise and golden crust. **PICTURED ON PAGES 192–3.**

6 egg yolks

120g caster sugar

I tsp salt

40g cornflour

500ml whole milk

seeds of 2 vanilla pods or 4 tsp vanilla extract

3 tbsp Camp coffee essence

25g toasted skinned hazelnuts, very finely chopped

For the choux pastry

80g plain flour

55g strong white flour

120ml whole milk

120ml water

I tsp fine salt

I tbsp caster sugar

120g butter

220–240g eggs (about 4–5 eggs), lightly beaten

To make the filling, put the egg yolks and sugar in a bowl with the salt and mix well together. Then mix in the cornflour until combined. Set aside.

Heat the milk in a pan with the vanilla until it is just about to boil, then take it off the heat. Drizzle about 3 tablespoons of the hot milk into the egg mixture and mix well to combine. Then add the rest of the milk, mixing again to combine. Pour the mixture back into the pan on a medium heat, stirring all the time until thickened and boiling.

Stir in the coffee essence and transfer to a bowl. Put a piece of baking parchment right on the surface of the mixture to prevent a skin from forming. Leave this to cool to room temperature, then chill for at least 4 hours or preferably overnight.

Preheat the oven to 150°C (fan 130°C/300°F/gas 2). To make the choux pastry, sift the flours onto a sheet of baking parchment. Put the milk, water, salt, sugar and butter in a small pan over a medium heat. Heat until the butter has melted. Then turn up the heat and bring it to the boil, stirring to ensure the salt and sugar have dissolved. As soon as it comes to a rolling boil, take it off the heat and tip in the flours, beating well with a wooden spoon for I minute. Then return the pan to the heat for another 2 minutes to 'cook out' the mixture a little – the dough should pull away from the sides of the pan, and you should see that a thin film has formed on the bottom of the pan. Leave to cool slightly, for about 3 minutes.

For choux pastry, the amount of egg you need changes from day to day according to the weather, the moisture in the air, the quality of your flour and how long you 'cooked out' your mixture – if you cooked it out a lot then your mixture will be dry and require more liquid.

COFFEE ECLAIRS WITH ESPRESSO & TOASTED HAZELNUT CREAM

For the next stage, you can either use a hand-held electric whisk or transfer the mixture to a bowl in a stand mixer fitted with a paddle attachment. When the mixture is at body temperature, add a quarter of the eggs and beat well until the mixture is combined. Then add another quarter and beat well again.

You will need to beat it pretty hard to get all of the mixture mixed in. Repeat with the next quarter of the eggs and beat again. Now you should have a quarter of the egg mixture left – add half of this and beat it well, until the pastry is smooth, shiny and has reached a piping consistency. Aim to include as much egg in the mixture as possible while still keeping the mixture to a 'reluctant dropping consistency', as this means the choux will rise and turn to a good darkish golden-brown colour in the oven.

Place the choux pastry in the piping bag. Line two large baking sheets with baking parchment, and add a blob of choux pastry underneath each corner to prevent the baking parchment from moving around in the oven. Pipe 10cm lengths of the choux, each about 2.5cm wide, onto the lined baking sheets, spacing them about 5cm apart. Apply an even pressure to the piping bag throughout the whole length of each éclair.

Bake for 55–60 minutes, checking it after 35–40 minutes to see how it looks – the choux pastry is done when it is slightly darker than golden brown and really quite firm and crisp, especially around the edges. After 45 minutes, open the oven door for about 10 seconds to allow some steam to escape and then close it again.

Once the éclairs are cooked, remove them from the oven and cut a little slit at the bottom of each one with a paring knife to release any steam. Leave them to cool down completely. While the eclairs are cooling down, remove the filling from the fridge and whisk it up again until nice and smooth, then fold in the toasted hazelnuts until evenly combined.

For the coffee glaze
280g white fondant icing (shop-bought)

1 tsp warm water

1 tsp Camp coffee essence

For the topping
30g toasted skinned hazelnuts, very finely chopped

Equipment
hand-held electric whisk or stand mixer

piping bag with 1.5cm star-shaped nozzle (choose one with prongs very close together to prevent cracking)

large piping bag

sugar thermometer

> To check that your choux pastry has reached the 'reluctant dropping consistency', scoop up a bit of the mixture on the wooden spoon, hold it horizontally and shake it once. If the mixture does not fall off the spoon you will need to add the rest of the egg. If it does fall off the spoon, then it is ready and you do not have to add the rest of the egg.

Use a skewer to make three small holes in the bottom of each éclair. Place the filling in the large piping bag and snip off a small opening. Pipe into the three holes until the filling starts to ooze out through them a little. The filled éclairs should feel heavy for their size. Repeat until all the éclairs have been filled.

Put all the ingredients for the coffee glaze in a heatproof bowl and mix until evenly combined. Put the bowl over a pan of gently simmering water with the sugar thermometer and stir constantly until the glaze reaches 35°C (95°F). Turn the éclairs upside down and then dip the top third of each éclair into the coffee glaze. Sweep off any excess glaze around the edges with your finger, and arrange them on a wire rack, glazed side up.

Once you have glazed a few éclairs, sprinkle some hazelnuts along the length of the glaze, gently pressing them into the still soft glaze to help them to stick. Leave the glaze to set for at least 10 minutes before serving. The glaze is best used at 35°C (95°F), so if it cools too much while you are dipping, place the bowl back over the simmering water until it has reached the correct temperature.

Once all of the éclairs are decorated, put them onto a plate and serve. The éclairs will keep in the fridge for up to 2–3 hours without going soggy.

TOASTED ALMOND MINI PAVLOVAS WITH RASPBERRIES & WHITE CHOCOLATE DRIZZLE

MAKES 18

Some people find meringue difficult to make, but I hope this recipe makes it easy! It just takes a good recipe, some eggs that are about a week old (but still in date), a little patience and a whole lot of whisking and your meringues are sure to be the shiniest in your street! The cornflour in the recipe helps the meringue to be a little chewy, which is customary for a Pavlova. **PICTURED ON PAGES 192–3.**

Preheat the oven to 180°C (fan 160°C/350°F/gas 4).

Put the flaked almonds (including 50g extra for the top, if using) into a baking tin. Cook in the oven for 6–8 minutes, until golden brown, shaking the tin once or twice to ensure they cook evenly. Remove from the oven and separate out into 150g and 50g amounts. Set aside until needed.

Reduce the oven temperature to 140°C (fan 120°C/275°F/gas 1). Line two baking sheets with baking parchment. Put the egg whites in a large bowl and whisk them until they begin to thicken and turn opaque – this should take a couple of minutes using a hand-held electric whisk or a stand mixer.

Add a quarter of the sugar and whisk up the egg whites again until the mixture goes stiff. Keep whisking the egg whites, and with the other hand, add the sugar in a steady stream, whisking all the time. This technique is called 'meringuing the foam', and is a quick and easy way to make beautiful meringue.

When you have added all the sugar, keep whisking the meringue until the mixture goes really stiff and shiny. To check that it is ready, take some of the meringue on the end of the whisk, then turn the whisk meringue-covered end up – the meringue should be super stiff and not floppy.

Using a spatula, fold in the cornflour, lemon juice and 150g toasted flaked almonds. Dab little blobs of the meringue under each corner of the baking parchment on the baking sheets. The meringue will act like glue, stopping your parchment from flying around in the oven.

Take a mechanical ice-cream scoop or a big metal spoon and put eighteen equal-sized dollops of the mixture onto the lined baking sheets, and then use a smaller spoon to make a big indent in the centre of each Pavlova shell. Once the Pavlovas are baked, the cream and fruit will sit in here.

150g flaked almonds, plus 50g extra for decorating (optional)

4 egg whites, at room temperature

225g caster sugar

1 tsp cornflour

squeeze of lemon juice

For the filling
300ml double cream

seeds of ½ vanilla pod or 1 tsp vanilla extract

60g icing sugar (sifted if lumpy)

To decorate
500g fresh raspberries

100g white chocolate, roughly chopped

Equipment
hand-held electric whisk or stand mixer

mechanical ice-cream scoop (optional)

disposable piping bag (optional)

Bake the Pavlovas for 1–1¼ hours or until they are firm to the touch. These should not go golden but they will colour very lightly to a pale yellow colour. Once baked, remove them from the oven and leave them to cool down completely.

Once the Pavlovas are cool, make the filling. Whisk up the double cream, vanilla and icing sugar in a bowl until the cream is just holding its shape. It is very easy to over-whisk the cream, so stop when it starts to thicken.

Place the Pavlova shells onto plates and then divide the flavoured cream between the shells. Place the raspberries on top. Scatter over the rest of the toasted flaked almonds, if you fancy it.

Melt the chocolate in a heatproof bowl set over a pan of simmering water. Make sure the base of the bowl does not touch the simmering water. You can also melt the chocolate in the microwave using 40-second blasts, stirring well between each blast so that the chocolate does not burn.

Use a disposable piping bag or simply use a fork to flick the melted chocolate over the raspberries. If you use a piping bag, go as neat or as freestyle as you fancy. Serve.

I like to use the ice-cream scoop to measure out the meringue mixture – it makes it easier to create shells of a similar size.

CHOCOLATE VOL-AU-VENTS WITH PECAN PRALINE CREME MOUSSELINE & RASPBERRIES

MAKES 6

It is rare to see crème mousseline these days unless you visit very fine patisseries. It is also called German buttercream and is essentially a crème pâtissière enriched with a whole lot of butter – incredibly decadent! It's good to have lots of different filling alternatives so you can really experiment with the look and feel of your beautiful baked goods. **PICTURED ON PAGES 192–3.**

Remove the chocolate puff pastry from the fridge and set aside.

To make the pecan praline, line a large baking sheet with baking parchment and spray a little oil on it, then set it aside. Put the sugar and water into a pan over a low heat and allow the sugar to dissolve. Have a pastry brush standing in a cup of hot water nearby and use this to brush down any sugar on the sides of the pan, as it may cause the mixture to crystallize into a lump.

Once the sugar has dissolved, turn up the heat and allow the mixture to boil. Keep it bubbling away for about 6 minutes, or until the mixture turns to the colour of honeycomb – not too dark as it will taste bitter. Once it is ready, take it off the heat. As soon as the bubbles have subsided a little, add the pecans, moving the pan around gently to swirl the mixture a little. Make sure all of the pecans are covered and then pour the mixture onto the lined baking sheet and set aside to cool down.

Once the mixture is cool and hard, pop it into a food processor and blitz, then set this aside. You don't want massive pieces but you don't want it to be blitzed into a powder either, so aim for small bite-sized chunks.

Line a large baking sheet with baking parchment. Roll out the chocolate puff pastry on a lightly floured surface until it is slightly thinner than a £1 coin (about 3mm). Then using the 9cm round cutter, stamp out rounds from the pastry, re-rolling if need be to get twelve rounds. Brush off any excess flour and then put six rounds on the baking sheet and set aside. Take the 5cm round cutter and cut out the centres of the remaining six rounds on the floured work surface. You will be using the large rings for this recipe, so set the 5cm cut-out rounds aside.

> I like to stack the 5cm puff-pastry cut-out centres carefully, wrap them in cling film and then pop them in the freezer for another recipe.

640g chocolate puff pastry (see page 273)

plain flour, for dusting

egg wash, for brushing

icing sugar, for dusting

18 raspberries, to decorate

For the pecan praline

a little oil, for spraying

50g granulated sugar

1 tbsp water

30g pecans, roughly chopped

For the crème mousseline

3 egg yolks

80g caster sugar

20g cornflour

250ml whole milk

1 vanilla pod, seeds scraped out

100g butter, softened and cut into cubes

Brush egg wash around the outside edge of the pastry rounds on the baking sheet, making sure that the egg does not run down the sides as this may stop the vol-au-vents from puffing up nicely in the oven. Place each pastry ring on top of an egg-washed round, to give you six vol-au-vents in total. Brush a little more egg wash all over the tops of the vol-au-vents, again making sure not to drip any down the sides. Pop these into the fridge to firm up for 30 minutes.

Preheat the oven to 220°C (fan 200°C/450°F/gas 7). After 30 minutes, remove the vol-au-vents from the fridge and criss-cross a little over the top of the pastry with a sharp knife. Glaze the vol-au-vents again with the egg wash and put them into the oven. Turn the oven temperature down to 180°C (fan 160°C/350°F/gas 4) and cook for 25–30 minutes, or until the vol-au-vents are well risen. Squeeze the outside of one – they should be quite firm.

As the puff pastry is cooking, make the crème mousseline. Put the egg yolks and caster sugar together in a bowl and whisk together well for a few minutes, until the mixture lightens to a much paler yellow. Once the mixture has reached this stage, add the cornflour and whisk very well again, then set it aside.

Put the milk and the vanilla pod and seeds in a pan over a medium–high heat until just boiling, then remove it from the heat and add one third of the milk to the egg yolk mixture, whisking well. Then add the rest of the milk to the egg yolk mixture and whisk again (you don't really want to get lots of air into it). Pour this mixture back into the same pan and put it on a medium–high heat, until it starts bubbling. Turn down the heat and cook through, stirring for a good 2–3 minutes to 'cook out' the cornflour as it thickens a little. Then put the mixture into the bowl of a stand mixer and beat on quite a low speed until it reaches body temperature. You can also use a hand-held electric whisk for this. Add the butter, bit by bit, beating well between each addition. Once all of the butter is added, tip in three-quarters of the praline and stir to combine.

Once the vol-au-vents are baked, remove them from the oven and sprinkle the tops with some icing sugar. Place them briefly under a hot grill for a few seconds, so that the icing sugar caramelizes to a nice sheen. Keep an eye on them as they can burn in super-quick time.

Half-fill the piping bag with praline crème mousseline and then pipe it into the vol-au-vent cases. I like to fill them pretty much up to the top. Put three raspberries on top of each vol-au-vent and then sprinkle over the remaining praline. Serve.

Equipment
food processor

9cm round cutter

5cm round cutter

stand mixer or hand-held electric whisk

piping bag with 1cm plain nozzle

VEGAN GINGER & DATE SPELT SCONES WITH BLACKCURRANTS

Most of us know someone who is vegan, and the struggles they face finding certain foods. Baked goods are always challenging, as most high-street bakers make delicacies that are laden with dairy. I created these scones for my vegan friends to enjoy, but I wanted them to be super tasty for anyone. Spelt is one of the oldest cultivated grains and has a naturally higher composition of vitamins.

Preheat the oven to 180°C (fan 160°C/350°F/gas 4) and line a baking sheet with baking parchment.

Put the flour and oats in a large bowl with the baking powder. Add the sunflower spread and lightly rub the mixture with your fingertips until the mixture resembles very fine breadcrumbs. Using a round-bladed knife, stir in the salt, ginger and dates. Make a well in the centre and pour in the almond milk and add the vanilla, if using, and again using the knife, quickly mix the ingredients together to form a dough. This process ensures that your scones do not get too tough and chewy.

Tip the mixture out onto a floured surface and roll the dough until it is about 1.5cm thick. If your mixture is quite sticky, sprinkle some extra flour on top. Using a lightly dusted cutter, stamp out eight scones and place them on the lined baking sheet. Try not to twist the cutter, otherwise your scones may not have a nice, straight rise. Scrunch up the excess dough, knead very gently until smooth and then re-roll to cut as many scones as possible.

Push about five frozen blueberries into each scone. I like to do it this way, as the berries can stain the dough red if they are mixed into the dough.

Place the scones on the lined baking sheet as you go – you may need to re-roll any trimmings to get the last scone. Glaze with the almond milk and scatter the flaked almonds on top, if using. Then bake for 15–20 minutes, or until the scones have risen and are a golden-brown colour.

Remove the scones from the oven and serve. These are best served warm or at least on the day that they are made.

310g white spelt flour, plus extra for dusting

50g porridge oats

2 tsp baking powder

80g pure sunflower spread, cold

pinch of sea salt flakes

2 tsp ground ginger

3 pitted dates, finely chopped

180ml almond milk, plus extra to glaze

seeds of ½ vanilla pod or 1 tsp vanilla extract (optional)

25g frozen blueberries

25g flaked almonds (optional)

Equipment

6.5cm fluted or straight-sided round cutter

GLUTEN-FREE CHOCOLATE ORANGE POLENTA CUPCAKES

MAKES 12

Finding decent substitutes for wheat flour is a challenge, and I have come to accept that the texture of gluten-free baked goods will always be slightly different. Often used for savoury dishes, polenta has a different texture to regular flour, but when used in the right way it can make lovely moist cupcakes.

Preheat the oven to 180°C (fan 160°C/350°F/gas 4) and line the muffin tin with twelve paper cases.

Put the butter and sugar in a bowl and cream together using a wooden spoon until it is light and fluffy. Once the mixture is really light, add the eggs, one at a time, beating well between each addition. The mixture can sometimes look a little curdled at this stage but it will come good. Fold in the ground almonds, cocoa powder, polenta, baking powder, orange zest and juice, and then finally fold in the chocolate chips, using as few stirs as possible.

Using a large spoon or a mechanical ice-cream scoop, divide the mixture between the cupcake cases. Then place a mandarin or satsuma segment on the top of each cupcake and push it down slightly. Bake in the oven for 25–30 minutes, or until cooked through and golden brown. To check that they are cooked, insert a skewer into the centre of a cupcake – it should come out clean.

Once the cupcakes are baked, remove the tin from the oven and serve them warm or cold.

220g butter, softened

220g soft light brown sugar

3 eggs

200g ground almonds

2 tbsp cocoa powder

100g fine polenta

1 tsp baking powder (gluten-free)

zest and juice of 1 large orange

50g dark chocolate chips

12 mandarin or satsuma segments, pith removed

Equipment

12-hole cupcake tin

mechanical ice-cream scoop (optional)

GLUTEN-FREE CLEMENTINE & ALMOND CAKE WITH POMEGRANATES

My friend Satya gave me her version of an orange cake when I went for tea at her house. The cake was rich and slightly bitter, but also sweet with the tang of orange that lasted well after you had finished the final bite. This is my version of her beautiful cake and I hope that I can do it justice. I've used clementines but you could replace them with two large oranges instead, boiling them for a little longer. It is best to serve this spongy cake while it is warm.

Preheat the oven to 180°C (fan 160°C/350°F/gas 4) and line the tin with baking parchment. Pop the clementines into a large pan, then cover with water and bring to the boil. Reduce the heat, then cover with a lid and simmer for 45 minutes, or until the clementines are super soft – this makes the clementines much less bitter. Allow the clementines to cool down a little and then put them into a food processor and blend to a smooth paste. Set aside.

Put the butter and sugar together in a large bowl and beat them well with the hand-held electric whisk until light and fluffy. Then add the honey and beat for another minute or so. Add two of the eggs and half of the ground almonds and beat until well combined and then add the other egg with the rest of the almonds along with the clementine puree, cinnamon and baking powder. Beat again until evenly combined. You can of course use a stand mixer to do this.

Tip the mixture into the lined tin and cover it loosely with foil. Pop the tin into the oven to bake for about 55–60 minutes, or until a skewer inserted into the centre of the cake comes out clean.

About 15 minutes before the cake is ready, make the orange syrup. Put the orange zest and juice in a small pan with the soft light brown sugar and place over a low heat until the sugar dissolves, stirring occasionally. Once the sugar has dissolved, turn up the heat and boil it for about 5 minutes, or until the orange syrup has thickened and reduced slightly. Set aside until needed.

Once the cake is baked, remove it from the oven and carefully take it out of the tin. Transfer to a cake stand or serving plate, and while it is still hot, brush the syrup all over the top and sides. I am generous with the syrup so that the cake is sticky, well soaked and full of flavour. Scatter the pomegranate seeds and flaked almonds over the cake and dust with icing sugar, if using. Transfer any leftover syrup to a little jug and serve with the cake.

5 medium clementines, scrubbed (but not peeled)

120g butter, softened

150g soft light brown sugar

50g honey

3 eggs

320g ground almonds

½ tsp ground cinnamon

1 tsp baking powder (gluten-free)

For the orange syrup

zest and juice of 1 large orange

150g soft light brown sugar

To decorate

large handful of pomegranate seeds

handful of toasted flaked almonds

icing sugar (optional)

Equipment

20cm round loose-bottomed cake tin, at least 7.5cm deep

food processor

hand-held electric whisk or stand mixer

GLUTEN-FREE MADEIRA LOAF CAKE

Madeira cake is traditionally made by creaming butter and sugar together first, and then adding the eggs and eventually the flour and almonds. I prefer to make a 'crumb' first, and then mix it with the eggs and water. I think this method is foolproof, and great if you are baking in a rush!

Preheat the oven to 180°C (fan 160°C/350°F/gas 4) and make sure the shelf in the middle of the oven is at the ready. Line the loaf tin with baking parchment – I usually put a strip along the whole length of the tin, making sure that it comes well over the edges. This makes it easy to remove the loaf when it is cooked.

Put the flour, almonds and sugar along with the butter and lemon zest into a food processor and pulse until the mixture resembles fine breadcrumbs. I find that this is the best way to make this cake, but if you do not have a food processor, you can also use your hands to 'rub' the mixture together, putting your hands in and rubbing the butter and flour mixture and then letting it fall back into the bowl.

Keep pulsing or rubbing the mixture until it resembles fine breadcrumbs. Lightly beat the eggs with the warm water in a jug and then add to the bowl or food processor and beat really well until it comes together.

Using a spatula, spoon the cake mixture into the loaf tin and bake in the oven for 50–55 minutes, or until a skewer inserted into the centre of the cake comes out clean. If the cake starts to go a little dark on top, just cover it with a piece of baking parchment.

Once the cake is cooked, remove it from the oven and leave it to cool completely in the tin. When it is cool, remove it from the tin, cut into slices and serve.

100g gluten-free self-raising flour (I like Doves Farm)

70g ground almonds

150g caster sugar

160g butter, cold and cut into cubes

zest of I lemon

3 eggs

2 tbsp warm water

Equipment

450ml loaf tin

food processor (optional)

GLUTEN-FREE BOILED ORANGE AND LEMON CAKE WITH HONEY

There are many traditional recipes for a boiled orange cake, and this is just my version of the beautiful Middle Eastern-inspired cake: moist, rich and gluten-free. This recipe does take a little longer to cook than other cake recipes, as you need to boil the citrus fruits to make them soft enough to blitz into a puree. If you wish to decorate your cake with a flower, make sure it is safe to use with food and not poisonous.

Pop the oranges into a large pan, then cover with water and bring to the boil. Reduce the heat, then cover with a lid and simmer for 1 hour, then add the lemon and cook for another 45 minutes. Drain off and discard the water, leaving you with just the fruit. Allow the oranges to cool down a little and then roughly chop and put them into a food processor with all of their juices. Blend them to a smooth puree and then set aside until needed.

Preheat the oven to 180°C (fan 160°C/350°F/gas 4) and line the tin with baking parchment. Put the caster sugar, honey and three of the eggs into a large bowl and whisk them together with a hand-held electric whisk until frothy. You can also do this with a hand whisk. When the mixture is frothy, add another two of the eggs with half of the ground almonds, the baking powder, cinnamon and cloves. Mix together using a wooden spoon until well combined. The mixture won't look great at this stage but soon all will be well. Add the remaining two eggs with the rest of the ground almonds and mix again to combine. Finally, using a spatula, quickly fold in the citrus puree until evenly mixed.

Pour the cake batter into the lined tin and bake for 35–40 minutes, until the cake is firm to the touch and a skewer inserted into the centre of the cake comes out clean.

When the cake is cooked, remove from the oven and leave to cool a little, then place a flat serving plate over the top of the cake tin. Holding both the cake tin and the plate, flip it over so that the cake tin is upside down. Put everything down on the worktop, release the springform tin and then lift it off.

If you wish to create the dusting design, place the doily on the top as a stencil, and then dust it with icing sugar and carefully remove the doily. The icing sugar will soak into the cake within 15 minutes, so do this just before serving. Top with a flower and a scattering of mint leaves, if you fancy it.

2 small oranges, scrubbed (but not peeled)

1 lemon, scrubbed (but not peeled)

200g caster sugar

80g honey

7 eggs

300g ground almonds

1 tsp baking powder (gluten-free)

2 tsp ground cinnamon

½ tsp ground cloves

To decorate

icing sugar, for dusting

handful of fresh small mint leaves (optional)

flower of your choice (optional)

Equipment

food processor

23cm springform cake tin

hand-held electric whisk (optional)

doily (optional)

GLUTEN-FREE CRANBERRY & OAT SODA BREAD

In 2007, a routine blood test showed that I had coeliac disease. Panic set in as I sunk into obsessive thoughts about all of the foods I would not be able to enjoy. But as is my way, I saw it as a challenge to use my skills as a baker to make the most delicious gluten-free baked goods and treats, such as this one. Months later, I found out that the initial diagnosis was incorrect, but I've continued to experiment with different flours and combinations.

Preheat the oven to 200°C (fan 180°C/400°F/gas 6) and place a baking sheet in the oven. If you're making your own buttermilk, put the milk and lemon juice in a jug and allow it to sit for 15 minutes.

Put the flour, oats, bicarbonate of soda and salt into a large bowl and mix together with a wooden spoon. Then add the egg yolks, treacle and cranberries. Make a well in the centre, then add enough of the buttermilk and mix to make a nice soft dough. You might not need all of the buttermilk, so just add enough so it comes together nicely and is not too wet.

Remove the baking sheet from the oven and sprinkle some flour over it, being careful as it will be hot. Get your hands in the bowl and bring the dough together with a couple of turns. Then turn out onto a lightly floured work surface and using your hands form the dough into a circle, about 18cm across and 5cm thick. Put the soda bread onto the heated baking sheet.

Being careful of the hot baking sheet, dip your wooden spoon into the bag of flour, and place it horizontally on the bread, pushing all the way down to the baking sheet to form the first half of the traditional cross. Change the direction of the spoon so it is at right angles to the other line and repeat this process to create a big cross. Take the extra oats and then sprinkle them over the top of the bread.

Bake the bread in the oven for 30–40 minutes, or until the bread is golden and crusty. To check that the bread is properly cooked, tap the base – it should sound hollow. The dough inside the cross should also be cooked and no longer wet. If the bread is not quite ready then place it back into the oven for another 5 minutes or so.

Once the bread is cooked, transfer it to a wire rack and leave to cool for 10 minutes. This bread is best eaten warm.

300ml buttermilk or 300ml whole milk with juice of ½ lemon

300g gluten-free plain white or brown flour, plus extra for dusting (I like Doves Farm)

100g gluten-free porridge oats, plus extra for sprinkling

1½ tsp bicarbonate of soda

I tsp salt

3 egg yolks

I tbsp black treacle (optional)

80g dried cranberries (can use another dried fruit also)

GLUTEN-FREE PARMESAN POLENTA MUFFINS WITH CHIVES & CHEDDAR

I would love to eat this savoury mufffin for breakfast on most days of the week. If you want to add a little spice to your mornings, throw in a couple of teaspoons of chilli flakes, I finely chopped fresh jalapeno or I teaspoon of chilli powder.

70ml butter, melted, plus extra for brushing

250g polenta

50g gluten-free self-raising flour (I like Doves Farm)

4 tbsp fresh chives, finely chopped

I tsp baking powder

50g Cheddar cheese, grated

pinch of salt

I egg

350ml Greek yoghurt

110ml whole milk

75g tinned sweetcorn, drained

30g Parmesan cheese, freshly grated

Equipment

12-hole muffin tin

mechanical ice-cream scoop (optional)

Preheat the oven to 200°C (fan 180°C/400°F/gas 6) and line the muffin tin with twelve paper cases. Brush each case with a little melted butter and set aside until needed.

Put the polenta, flour, chives, baking powder, Cheddar and salt into a bowl and mix everything together using a wooden spoon. Then add the egg, yoghurt, milk, melted butter and sweetcorn and mix together. Divide the mixture evenly between the twelve paper cases, using a mechanical ice-cream scoop or two large spoons. Sprinkle over the Parmesan and then bake for 25–30 minutes, or until a skewer inserted into the centre of the muffins comes out clean.

Once baked, remove the muffins from the oven and leave to cool a little. These are great served warm or cold, but they are best served on the day they are made.

REFINED SUGAR-FREE APRICOT, ORANGE & ALMOND FLAPJACKS

So many recipes and cookbooks out there claim to be sugar-free, but still include a lot of honey. I don't understand that – honey is a type of sugar and your body reacts pretty much the same way to it as it does to all the usual suspects. Dried fruit and regular fruit are packed with sugar, but they have a redeeming quality: due to their fibre content, the insulin spike that comes with eating sugar is reduced somewhat, making them slightly healthier.

Preheat the oven to 180°C (fan 160°C/350°F/gas 4) and line the baking tin with baking parchment. I make sure there is some extra baking parchment hanging over the edges – this makes it easier to pull out the flapjacks once they are ready.

Spread the almonds out in a small baking tray and cook in the oven for 3–4 minutes, or until lightly toasted. Keep an eye on them as they do catch quickly. Remove them from the oven and leave to cool.

Put the dates in a blender (or you can use the smaller bowl of a food processor if you have that attachment) and add the water and blitz to a paste. Tip this into a large bowl along with the toasted almonds, oats, apricots, orange, salt, cinnamon, vanilla, and sesame, sunflower and pumpkin seeds. Mix to combine and then mix in the coconut oil or butter.

Tip the mixture into the lined tin and squish down with a wooden spoon – spending a little bit of time doing this will stop the flapjacks from falling apart when you cut them. I use my full body weight to really push down on it! Using a sharp knife, mark out sixteen squares and pop the flapjacks into the oven for 18–20 minutes.

When the flapjacks are baked, remove them from the oven and leave them to cool a little bit, then carefully remove from the tin using the overhanging baking parchment. Cut into the sixteen squares to serve.

100g blanched almonds, finely chopped

175g pitted dates (Medjool or any sticky dates are good)

240ml water

250g porridge oats

100g ready-to-eat dried apricots, finely chopped

zest of ½ orange

pinch of sea salt flakes

pinch of ground cinnamon

seeds of 1 vanilla pod or 2 tsp vanilla extract

50g sesame seeds

50g sunflower seeds

50g toasted pumpkin seeds

3 tbsp melted extra-virgin coconut oil or 3 tbsp melted butter

Equipment

20cm square cake tin

blender or food processor

Why not change the apricots to your favourite dried fruit and substitute the almonds with another nut – hazelnuts or pistachios would also be delicious.

REFINED SUGAR-FREE WALNUT & RASPBERRY ONE-BOWL BROWNIES

This is a shortcut brownie recipe, perfect for when you just want to pull something together in super-quick time, without the need for whisking and folding. All you need is a food processor and about 10 minutes, and the big bonus is that they just happen to contain no refined sugar – not that you'd notice, as they are so delicious.

Preheat the oven to 180°C (fan 160°C/350°F/gas 4) and line the tin with baking parchment. I make sure there is some extra baking parchment hanging over the edges – this makes it easier to pull out the brownies when they are baked.

Melt the butter in a small pan or in the microwave and then leave to cool a little. Put the flour in a food processor with the dates, baking powder, cocoa powder, milk, eggs and melted butter. Then blitz until the mixture comes together and is well combined.

Tip the walnuts and 100g of the raspberries into the mixture and use a spoon or spatula to mix it together. Spoon this mixture into the lined tin, using the back of a spoon to make sure the top is nice and smooth. Arrange the remaining 50g of the raspberries on top, pushing them down ever so slightly into the mixture.

Pop this baking tin onto a baking sheet (this makes it easier to move the tin around) and then bake for about 15 minutes. When cooked it should be dry on top, but still slightly gooey and fudgy inside. Don't be tempted to leave it in the oven any longer than this, or you may end up with cake, not brownies – although they will still taste delicious!

Once the brownies are cooked, remove them from the oven, allow to cool a little in the tin and then cut into nine large squares. They are delicious served warm or cold.

110g butter

75g plain flour or white spelt flour

170g pitted dates, chopped (Medjool or any that look soft and sticky)

1 tsp baking powder

70g cocoa powder (sifted if lumpy)

70ml whole milk

2 eggs

80g walnuts, roughly chopped

150g raspberries

Equipment

20cm square cake tin

food processor

CELEBRATION

GINGER & CINNAMON STAINED GLASS WINDOW COOKIES

I wrap these cookies up for Christmas presents and love to hang them on the tree for decorations. They are really pretty with the colourful sweet fillings. If you want to hang them you'll need lengths of coloured ribbon. The beauty of these cookies is that they last for quite some time. I love their flavour, but increase the amount of ginger if you would like them extra spicy. Bake any leftover cookie shapes in the oven for 4–6 minutes, until firm.

100g butter

100g soft light brown sugar

2 tbsp golden syrup

1 tsp treacle

1 tbsp ground ginger

1 tbsp ground cinnamon

large pinch of ground cloves

pinch of chilli powder (optional)

½ tsp bicarbonate of soda

250g plain flour

5 plain boiled sweets (in different colours), roughly chopped

Equipment

9cm star or snowflake-shaped cutter

4cm star or snowflake-shaped cookie cutter

2cm star or snowflake-shaped cookie cutter (optional)

Preheat the oven to 200°C (fan 180°C/400°F/gas 6). Line two large baking sheets with baking parchment. Put the butter, sugar, golden syrup, treacle and spices into a pan over a gentle heat. Cook for 3–4 minutes, allowing the butter and sugar to melt and dissolve, stirring from time to time. Then remove from the heat and stir in the bicarbonate of soda and flour in batches, stirring well between each addition, until you have a smooth, fairly stiff dough.

Allow the dough to cool down for a few minutes, so it is easy to roll out. Roll out the dough in between two large sheets of baking parchment to the thickness of a £1 coin (about 3mm), and then use the 9cm star or snowflake cutter to stamp out the large shapes. Scrunch up and re-roll the dough a few times to get 20–25 cookies.

Put the large cookies onto a baking sheet as you go. Once you have cut out all the large cookies, take the 4cm star or snowflake-shaped cookie cutter and stamp out the centre of the large shapes. You can put these small shapes onto a plate or another lined baking sheet to cook off later, if you fancy it. Otherwise, you could create a little floating star or snowflake in the centre of your cookies by stamping small shapes from the cut-out centres using the 2cm cutter. Place these little shapes (if using) inside the large cookie shapes.

Using a separate colour for each cookie, sprinkle a little of the chopped boiled sweets into the centre of each large star or snowflake, or, around the outside of the little shapes, if using. Using the tip of a wooden skewer, make a hole at the top of each shape.

Bake the cookies in the oven for 6–8 minutes, until going firm and beginning to darken, and the boiled sweet has melted to fill the hole. Remove them from the oven and, before they set, use the wooden skewer again to widen the ribbon hole a little more. Leave them to cool completely, and then serve.

FORTUNE COOKIES

I was thinking about what I should post on Instagram for Chinese New Year, aside from one of my tasty Chinese-influenced dishes. Fortune cookies sprang to mind. Although the method is a little fiddly, it is easy once you have had a few attempts. They are great for a party, especially as you can put your own messages inside! You can make only three of these cookies at a time, as they need shaping while they are warm. **PICTURED ON PAGE 218.**

Preheat the oven to 180°C (fan 160°C/350°F/gas 4). Cut out eighteen pieces of paper, each 6 x 1cm in size, and write different fortunes on them. You can also download and print these from the internet.

Line a baking sheet with baking parchment or use a non-stick silicone baking mat – I just love these as they make recipes like this so much easier to master. Melt the butter in a small pan or in the microwave and set aside to cool.

Put the egg whites and sugar in a bowl and mix together with a wooden spoon. You do not need lots of air in the mixture, as these cookies should not really rise in the oven. Add the flour and mix together to just combine and then add the melted butter with the salt and vanilla and mix together again to form a batter.

Take 1 tablespoon of the batter and place it onto the mat or lined baking sheet and then using the back of a metal spoon or a palette knife, spread the mixture evenly into a round, about 8cm wide. Keep spreading round and round with the spoon until it forms a disc. Repeat this process twice more so you have three rounds on the baking sheet. Pop these into the oven and cook them for 7–9 minutes, until cooked through and the edges have just started to turn a little darker.

While they are cooking, get a mug ready, along with a palette knife and the muffin tin.

When the cookies are ready, remove them from the oven and leave them for about 10 seconds, then very gently and carefully run a palette knife underneath one to loosen it from the baking parchment, pushing down on the baking sheet so that the edge of the knife does not go through the cookie. Quickly place a message into the middle of the cookie and fold the cookie in

50g butter

2 egg whites

100g caster sugar

50g white spelt or plain flour

pinch of salt

few drops of vanilla extract

Equipment

non-stick silicone baking mat (optional)

12-hole muffin tin

half over the top to create a half-moon shape, sealing the edges by squeezing them together with your fingers. Lift the cookie off the sheet and place the folded edge of the cookie onto the rim of the mug. Gently pull the corners down, one on the inside of the mug and one on the outside, to form the classic fortune cookie shape. Transfer this into one of the holes in the muffin tin so it can harden and keep its shape without springing back. Quickly repeat with the other cookies and set aside to cool.

Continue with the rest of the mixture, making three at a time, until you have used it all up. If you are using baking parchment, it is best to replace it between each batch otherwise the cookies tend to stick to it – this is why it is easier to use a non-stick silicone mat.

When you have made all of the fortune cookies, pile them onto a plate and serve. I like to make these on the day that I need them.

BOILED AND BAKED CHRISTMAS CAKE WITH GOJI BERRIES & DATES

I used to think that boiled fruit cakes never actually went into the oven. However, this isn't the case – the fruit is first boiled and then goes into the mixture and is baked in the usual way, but the preparation is considerably quicker and easier than making a regular fruitcake. Give it a go! It's a great short-cut version, perfect for those of us who are pressed for time.

Put the dates, cranberries, goji berries or raisins, blueberries and apricots into a pan with the water, butter and sugar and cook over a medium heat for 15 minutes, stirring occasionally. When the mixture is cooked, set it aside to cool to room temperature. This will take about half an hour.

Meanwhile, preheat the oven to 150°C (fan 130°C/300°F/gas 2) and line the cake tin with baking parchment, making sure there is excess hanging over the sides.

When the fruit mixture is cool, add the eggs, flour, almonds, baking powder, and spices and mix together to just combine. Transfer the mixture into the tin and then make a slight dip using a wooden spoon in the middle of the mixture – this helps the cake to rise more evenly. Pop the cake into the oven and bake for 45 minutes. Reduce the oven temperature to 140°C (fan 120°C/275°F/gas 1) and bake for another 45 minutes, or until risen, golden brown and a skewer inserted into the centre of the cake comes out clean. Remove from the oven.

About 10 minutes before the cake is cooked, spread the pecans out in a baking tin and slide them into the oven. Cook them until they are just toasted and then remove. Set aside to cool.

While the cake is still warm, brush the top generously with the apricot jam and arrange the toasted pecan nuts with the glacé cherries on top of the cake as per the picture. Brush the nuts and cherries with some more of the apricot jam and then leave the cake to cool completely.

When the cake is cool, wrap it in baking parchment and overwrap with foil. If time allows, leave in a cool dark place for about 3–7 days, then cut into slices to serve.

> If you fancy adding booze then prick the surface of the baked cake with a fine skewer and splash over 2–4 tbsp bourbon whiskey or rum. Leave to soak for about 1 hour.

100g pitted dates, chopped (I like Medjool)

50g dried cranberries

50g goji berries or raisins

50g dried blueberries

75g dried apricots, chopped

150ml water

150g butter

160g soft light brown sugar

3 eggs

100g white spelt flour

80g ground almonds

½ tsp baking powder

2 tsp ground allspice

2 tsp ground cinnamon

For the topping

75g pecans

100g apricot jam

100g glacé cherries

Equipment

20cm round loose-bottomed cake tin, at least 7.5cm deep

CHOCOLATE FRUIT, HAZELNUT & ALMOND SIMNEL CAKE

Simnel cakes are light fruit cakes that are traditionally made at Easter. Many people in my family are not fans of rich fruit cake, but throw some chocolate in and then they come running for it! I hope you like this twist on the traditional. Use whatever dried fruits and nuts you prefer, just keep the quantities the same.

Preheat the oven to 180°C (fan 160°C/350°F/gas 4) and line the cake tins with baking parchment. Put the butter, caster sugar, sour cream, eggs, flour, cocoa powder, baking powder, hazelnuts and almonds into a large bowl. In another bowl, mix the raisins with the extra 2 tablespoons flour.

Tip this raisin and flour mixture into the main bowl and beat together with a wooden spoon until well combined. Then, using a spatula, divide the cake mixture between the lined tins and level the tops. Bake on the middle shelf of the oven for 25–30 minutes, or until a skewer inserted into the centre of each cake comes out clean, and the cakes have shrunk slightly from the edges of the tin. Once the cakes are cooked, remove them from the oven and leave to cool completely in the tins.

When the cakes have cooled, make the chocolate icing. Melt the chocolate in a bain-marie by setting a heatproof bowl over a small pan of simmering water, making sure that the water in the pan does not touch the base of the bowl. If it does it can 'seize', making the chocolate very grainy and unpleasant to use. You can also melt the chocolate in the microwave in 40-second blasts, stirring well after each blast until smooth. Set the melted chocolate aside to cool a little. Now, put the butter in a bowl with the icing sugar and beat together until light and fluffy, then add the slightly cooled, melted chocolate to the mixture little by little, mixing to combine as you go.

Remove the cakes from the tins and place one on a serving plate with a blob of the chocolate icing underneath to stop it from moving around. Spread with a nice thick layer of the chocolate icing and then place the other cake on top, bottom side up so that it is nice and flat.

> I like to mix the raisins with flour before adding them to the mixture – this helps to stop the fruit from sinking to the bottom of the cake as it bakes.

150g butter, softened

220g caster sugar

120g sour cream

4 eggs

180g self-raising flour, plus extra 2 tbsp, for dusting the raisins

40g cocoa powder (sifted if lumpy)

½ tsp baking powder

100g toasted skinned hazelnuts, finely chopped

20g toasted blanched almonds, finely chopped

100g raisins

300g white marzipan

100g dark chocolate, roughly chopped, plus extra for shavings, if desired

For the chocolate icing

70g dark chocolate, roughly chopped

120g butter, softened

100g icing sugar, plus extra for dusting

Equipment

2 x 20cm round cake tins

>

CHOCOLATE FRUIT, HAZELNUT & ALMOND SIMNEL CAKE

Spread the top of the cake with a thin layer of the chocolate icing and then set this aside. You will also need to reserve about 1 tablespoon of the icing to stick the chocolate covered marzipan balls on top of your lovely cake!

Dust the work surface with a little icing sugar and then roll out two-thirds of the marzipan to the thickness of a £1 coin (about 3mm). Using a small sharp knife, put the 20cm round cake tin on top and use it as a stencil for a circle of marzipan.

Remove the cake tin and set aside and then place this marzipan circle on top of the cake, pressing it down with a little gentle pressure. You want it to be nice and smooth and even. Then crimp the edges to decorate using your thumb and forefinger, or you can just mark the cake around with a fork for a pretty pattern.

Line a baking sheet with baking parchment and set this aside. Melt the 100g chocolate over a bain-marie or in the microwave, as before. Leave to cool a little and then roll the rest of the marzipan into eleven equal-sized balls.

Take a marzipan ball on a fork and dip it into the melted chocolate, then remove it, letting the excess drip back into the bowl. Place the chocolate-coated marzipan ball on the baking parchment. Repeat with the rest of the balls and then, using small blobs of chocolate icing, stick the balls around the cake, equal-distance apart.

When you are ready to serve, lightly dust the Simnel cake with the icing sugar. You can also sprinkle over chocolate shavings, if you fancy it.

BLACK TOP & BOTTOM GANACHE LAYERED CAKE WITH TOASTED MERINGUE

When I worked in Hummingbird Bakery in London we made a black bottom cupcake. I always chuckled when I heard someone mention the name (for obvious reasons!). I had the idea to turn this black bottom cupcake into a black top and bottom layer cake with a white sponge in the middle, covered in a meringue that gets blasted with a blowtorch … and here it is!

235g butter, softened

220g dark chocolate (at least 70% cocoa solids), roughly chopped

4 eggs

180g self-raising flour

350g soft light brown sugar

2 tbsp cocoa powder (sifted if lumpy)

2 tbsp water

1–2 tsp black food colouring (optional and the amount depends on the brand you use)

For the white sponge layer

125g butter, softened

110g caster sugar

2 eggs

150g self-raising flour

1 egg white

3 tbsp crème fraiche

For the chocolate ganache

400ml double cream

Preheat the oven to 180°C (fan 160°C/350°F/gas 4). Line the cake tins with baking parchment and then set aside.

First make the chocolate sponge layers. Melt the butter in a pan over a low-medium heat and then remove the pan from the heat and add the chocolate, leaving it for a few minutes to melt. Once the chocolate has melted, stir the mixture until smooth and leave to cool down to room temperature.

Put the melted chocolate mixture into a large bowl and add the eggs, flour, soft light brown sugar, cocoa powder and water. Whisk well to combine and then add enough of the black food colouring to get a black batter, if using. You can do this in a stand mixer or using a hand-held electric whisk. You can also do this by hand, but it does take time and lots of elbow grease! Divide the batter between two of the lined cake tins and place them in the oven for 25–30 minutes, or until a skewer inserted into the centre of each cake comes out clean. Once they are baked, remove from the oven and leave them to cool completely.

While the chocolate cakes are cooking, make the white sponge mixture. Cream together the butter and the caster sugar until really light and fluffy. Add one of the eggs and half of the flour to the creamed butter and sugar, and mix well to combine. Add the remaining egg with the egg white, the rest of the flour and the crème fraiche and then mix again to combine. Tip the white sponge mixture into the remaining lined cake tin and bake in the oven for 25–30 minutes, or until a skewer inserted into the centre of the cake comes out clean. Remove it from the oven and leave to cool completely.

The black food colouring is an optional addition to give you a super black sponge. I must say against the white of the meringue it does look pretty cool. But if you don't fancy it the cake will still look great.

>

BLACK TOP & BOTTOM GANACHE LAYERED CAKE WITH TOASTED MERINGUE

375g dark chocolate (at least 70% cocoa solids), roughly chopped

For the meringue coating
225g granulated sugar

4 egg whites

Equipment
3 x 20cm round loose-bottomed cake tins

hand-held electric whisk or stand mixer

kitchen blowtorch

When the white sponge is in the oven, make the chocolate ganache. Put the cream into a pan and heat it up over a medium heat until it is boiling. Put the chocolate into a bowl and then pour the boiling cream over it. Leave it to sit for a couple of minutes and then carefully stir it all together with a spatula, using as few stirs as possible.

Once the ganache has cooled and thickened to a spreadable consistency, put a dollop on a serving plate or cake stand. Then put one of the chocolate sponge layers on top and spread over some of the ganache, then repeat with the white sponge layer with another layer of ganache on top. Finish with the remaining chocolate sponge and then spread the whole cake all over with the rest of the ganache. Once the cake is covered with a nice even layer of the chocolate ganache, put it in a cool place to firm up.

Meanwhile, make the meringue coating. Put the sugar into a large bowl and then add two of the egg whites and whisk them up until the mixture is stiff and shiny – this can take several minutes. Add another egg white and whisk it up again until stiff and shiny. Repeat this a final time with the remaining egg white and continue to whisk until it is stiff and shiny. The best way to do this is with a stand mixer with a whisk attachment, but a hand-held electric whisk is also good.

Using a large palette knife, slather the meringue all over the cake – I like it to look like soft butter on a piece of toast, rather than a covering of spikes or sharp points. When the cake is completely covered, take a blowtorch and run it over the cake. Keep it moving back and forward all of the time so that the meringue does not burn but turns golden brown all over.

Leave it to cool down a little before serving.

When you start to cover the cake with ganache, you may find that the crumb spreads into the ganache – if this happens, just put the whole cake in the fridge for 20 minutes or so to firm up before continuing to cover the cake.

FRAISIER CAKE WITH PORT & VANILLA

This recipe is stunning, although it does require some time to prepare. I recommend setting aside a rainy summer's afternoon to really enjoy the process of making something beautiful. The filling is crème diplomat (diplomat cream), which is a crème pâtissière with whipped cream added to lighten it. Some fraisier cakes are made with rich crème mousseline. As my recipe includes the strong flavour of port, diplomat cream is a better choice.

Preheat the oven to 180°C (160°C fan/350°F/gas 4) and line the baking trays with baking parchment. If you don't have baking trays this large, the trays that come with your oven will normally be of a similar size. The key is to be able to cut out a 22cm disc from both of the sponges.

First make the genoise sponges. Fill a medium pan a quarter full with water and bring it to the boil. Once it is boiling, remove it from the heat. Put the eggs into a bowl and set the bowl over the pan. Make sure that the pan is not too full, as you don't want any water splashing into the bowl.

Keep the pan off the heat and whisk up the eggs until they begin to thicken. I like to use a hand-held electric whisk for this. Add one quarter of the sugar (65g) and whisk again until all of the sugar has dissolved and the mixture is getting thicker. Continue to whisk the mixture, adding 65g sugar at a time until you have used up all the sugar. You want the mixture to reach ribbon stage, which should take 5–10 minutes or so from the first addition of sugar. To check that it has reached the right stage, lift up some of the mixture on the whisk and let it fall back down – it should sit on the surface of the mixture for about 5 seconds before slowly disappearing back in.

Pour the melted butter into the bowl, tipping it around the sides of the bowl so as not to knock out all of the air you have just whisked into your lovely mixture. Using a spatula, fold in the butter, using as few stirs as possible to keep the air in.

Once the butter is almost all mixed in, add a third of the flour, then carefully fold this in. I find that the trick is to do this quickly, keeping as much of the air in as possible. Repeat twice more to add the rest of the flour, making sure you fold in all of the flour as it can sometimes fall to the bottom of the bowl. Once you are happy with your mixture, divide the sponge mixture between the two lined baking trays.

For the genoise sponge
6 eggs

260g caster sugar

115g butter, melted

260g plain flour

For the strawberries
750g strawberries (about 500g equal-sized ones for outside the cake and 250g for inside the cake)

2 tbsp icing sugar

2 tbsp ruby red port

For the diplomat cream
10.5g leaf gelatine leaves

9 egg yolks

180g caster sugar

60g cornflour

750ml whole milk

seeds of 2 vanilla pods or 3 tsp vanilla extract

300ml whipping cream

Equipment
2 x 24 x 35cm rectangular baking trays

hand-held electric whisk

22cm cake ring

disposable piping bag

>

FRAISIER CAKE WITH PORT & VANILLA

Use a large palette knife to make them nice and even, but be light-handed with the palette knife so that the air stays in the cakes. Then pop them into the oven for 12–15 minutes, or until the sponges are cooked through, golden brown in colour and have just started to shrink slightly from the edges of the trays. Set the cakes aside to cool down completely.

To prepare the strawberries, first of all set aside 500g large equal-sized berries for around the outside of the cake. Then take the remaining 250g strawberries, cut off the green stems and cut them into bite-sized pieces. Place them in a bowl with the icing sugar and port. Mix these together and place in the fridge covered with cling film.

For the diplomat cream, put the gelatine leaves in a bowl and cover with cold water, then set aside to soak so that they become really soft. As the gelatine is soaking, mix the egg yolks and sugar together well in a large bowl, whisking them up until they are just a little light and fluffy – they don't need much air in them. Then add the cornflour, mix to combine and set this aside.

Heat the milk with the seeds of one vanilla pod or 2 teaspoons of vanilla extract in a medium pan until just before boiling, and then remove from the heat. Pour 1–2 tablespoons of this milk mixture into the egg mixture and whisk (again, it does not need any air whisked into it), then add the rest of the milk in a steady stream, whisking all the time until the mixture is uniform.

Pour the egg–milk mixture back into the pan that you used to heat the milk, and return this pan to the heat. Stirring all the time, cook the 'pastry cream' for 3–4 minutes until simmering. This process thickens the pastry cream and 'cooks out' any starchy flavour from the cornflour.

Remove the gelatine from the bowl and squeeze out, discarding as much of the water as you can. Add the softened gelatine to the hot mixture. Take the pan off the heat and then keep stirring it all the time to make sure that the gelatine completely dissolves into the pastry cream. Once it is dissolved, pour the cream into a bowl to cool down, covering it with baking parchment on the surface so that a skin does not form.

Once the pastry cream has cooled down, whip the cream along with the rest of the vanilla until you reach soft peaks. It needs to be a similar texture to the pastry cream. Remove the baking parchment from the pastry cream and add half of the whipped cream to it, whisking it together to combine. Using a spatula, fold in the remaining cream. Once everything is all mixed in, cover your cream and set it aside – this is now called diplomat cream.

Now it's time for the assembly! Take a sponge and place it sponge-side down and baking parchment-side up onto a large chopping board. Peel off the baking parchment. Take the cake ring and place it on the sponge – you may be able to simply press down and cut out the sponge circle, but if that does not work, you can use a sharp knife to cut around the outside of the ring. Then set the circle aside. You could save the cake scraps for another use, such as for cake pops or trifle (they will freeze for up to a month).

Take the second sponge and turn it upside down and parchment-side up onto the chopping board. Peel off the baking parchment and cut out another circle as above. Set this aside, saving the cake scraps for another use.

Take a large flat baking sheet and line it with baking parchment. Line the sides of your cake ring with baking parchment and place it on top of the lined baking sheet.

Remove the strawberries from the macerating liquid, and set them aside, reserving the liquid. Put one of the sponge layers inside the ring and then brush about half of the macerating liquid all over the top of the sponge.

Take half of the whole reserved large strawberries, cut off the green stems and cut them in half. Place the halves all the way around the inner edge of the ring so that the cut sides are facing outwards and the pointy ends are upwards. Place them really neatly and close together for the prettiest result – use a palette knife to help place them if you need to.

Setting aside one third of the diplomat cream for the top, put the rest into the piping bag and snip the tip to give a 1cm opening. Pipe the top of the large sponge with the diplomat cream. Continue to pipe the cream up the sides of the ring, being sure to get the mixture between the tops of the strawberries and at an even thickness all the way around. Place the macerated strawberries on top of the cream neatly in an even layer.

Place the second sponge circle on top of the macerated berries. Brush the sponge evenly with the rest of the reserved macerating liquid. Top with the diplomat cream all the way to the top of the cake ring, using a large flexible palette knife to make sure the top is flat and even. Now place the gateau in the fridge for at least 2–3 hours to set.

When you are ready to serve, remove the cake from the fridge. Rub the cake ring with your hands to warm it, and then lift it off. Top with the remaining strawberries, cutting them in half and leaving the green tops on for colour if you like. Serve.

LAVENDER OMBRE CAKE WITH PETAL ICING

Like all great show-stopper bakes, this cake requires some time and commitment to get the sponge colours and layers just so, and to pipe the icing in a way that is neat and level. Of course, if you don't have the patience for this simple 'petal' icing technique, then just spread your cake with the frosting, pile some blueberries on top and dust with icing sugar.

Preheat the oven to 180°C (fan 160°C/350°F/gas 4) and line the base of the tins with baking parchment.

Cream together the butter and caster sugar until light and fluffy. You can do this for 5 minutes in a stand mixer or using a hand-held electric whisk. You can also do this by hand, but it takes about 10 minutes and lots of elbow grease! Add four eggs and half of the flour to the creamed butter and sugar and beat well together. Then add the remaining eggs and the rest of the flour and salt and beat well again until well combined.

Divide the mixture into five small bowls, weighing each one to make sure it is even (you need about 350g per bowl). Now it is time to colour the ombre sponges, so they range from dark to light. I like to start with the darkest one first and get that a good purple colour. Remember that the purple will go a little darker when it bakes but not too much. Keep the lightest bowl as white batter, so you only need to colour four of the bowls. When you are happy with your colours, spoon the batters into your lined tins, using a spatula to scrape the bowls so you don't waste a drop of the batter. Spread the mixture evenly in the tins and bake the cakes in the oven (in batches if necessary) for 25–30 minutes, or until a skewer inserted into the centre of each cake comes out clean. Once the cakes are baked, gently turn them out onto wire racks to cool and peel off the baking parchment.

While the cakes are cooling, make the frosting. Put the butter into the stand mixer and beat well until very soft and light. Add the icing sugar in four goes, beating well between each addition. Cover the mixer with a tea towel so that the icing sugar does not fly everywhere.

Once the butter and the icing sugar are well combined, add the cream cheese and vanilla and then beat until just combined. Place 325g of the frosting in

450g butter, softened

450g caster sugar

9 eggs

450g self-raising flour

pinch of salt

1–2 tsp purple food colouring paste (I always use Sugarflair)

For cream cheese frosting

450g butter, softened

1kg icing sugar

450g cream cheese (I use Philadelphia)

2 tsp vanilla extract

1–2 tsp purple food colouring paste (I always use Sugarflair)

Equipment

5 x 20cm round cake tins

stand mixer

5 x disposable piping bags

>

LAVENDER OMBRE CAKE WITH PETAL ICING

one bowl and set it aside for crumb-coating the cake. Divide the remaining frosting into five small bowls, so you have 300g in four of the bowls and 350g in one bowl. Colour the 350g frosting the darkest shade of purple, then three of the other bowls in graduating colours as you did for the cake batter. Leave one bowl of frosting as it is. When the colour is even, pop each buttercream into a separate piping bag. Secure each bag with an elastic band and then put them in the fridge to firm up just a little so that they will be easier to pipe.

Once the cakes have cooled and the frostings have firmed a little, put all five cakes on the work surface, flat-sides up. Cut off the end of each piping bag, making sure each hole is the same size. Smear a splodge of the white frosting on your cake stand or plate to secure the white sponge. Spread a thin layer of the white frosting on the white sponge, spreading it to the very edge. Place the lightest purple sponge on top and spread with the corresponding coloured icing. Repeat with the other sponge layers, leaving the darkest sponge on top uncovered. Place the piping bags back in the fridge to keep firm.

Using the 325g reserved plain frosting, give the whole of the outside of the cake a crumb-coating. To do this, use a palette knife to spread a very thin layer of the frosting over the top and sides so that the whole cake is completely covered. Place the crumb-coated cake in the fridge to set for 10–15 minutes.

To create the ombre effect, take the piping bag filled with the plain buttercream and pipe a dot of the frosting on the bottom cake layer, easing the pressure on the piping bag when the dot is the same width as the bottom white cake layer. Place a small off-set spatula in the middle of the dot, then press down and drag the frosting left for only a centimetre. Wipe your spatula. Using the lightest purple frosting, pipe another dot directly above the first dot, and then press down and drag again, before wiping the spatula. Continue all the way up the cake until you have used all five buttercreams and have an ombre column running all the way up the cake. Then repeat this process all the way around the cake, overlapping the 'drag' of each dot as you go. You won't be able to drag the final column of dots, but this will be the back of the cake and you'll find that you won't even notice it.

Use the remaining frosting to pipe a circular ombre pattern on the top of the cake. Start with the darkest purple, and using the same dot, drag and wipe method, create a ring of icing around the edge of the cake. Make sure the ring meets the top layer of the icing on the sides of the cake. Repeat with the other frostings, finishing with just a small amount of the plain frosting at the centre. Allow the icing to set for about 10 minutes, and serve.

RUM & COCONUT CAKE WITH TOASTED COCONUT FLAKES

The first time I enjoyed this pairing of flavours, it was not in the form of a cake! In my early 20s, I enjoyed the tipple of a Malibu and cola: the perfect mix of coconut, rum and sugar. This cake refines the famous flavour combination. If you wish, you can omit the splash of rum in the sugar syrup. This cake is super-super sweet.

250g large coconut flakes, to cover

250g butter, softened

300g caster sugar

50g crème fraiche

300g self-raising flour

½ tsp baking powder

6 eggs

For the syrup

150g caster sugar

100ml water

2–3 tbsp dark rum (optional)

For the buttercream frosting

350g butter, softened

700g icing sugar (sifted if lumpy)

Equipment

3 x 20cm round cake tins

stand mixer or hand-held electric whisk

Preheat the oven to 200°C (fan 180°C/400°F/gas 6) and line the base of the tins with baking parchment.

To toast the coconut covering, place the coconut flakes onto a baking tray and place into the oven for 2–3 minutes, or until the coconut flakes are going golden brown. Then remove from the oven and set aside to cool.

To make the sponge, cream together the butter and caster sugar until light and fluffy. You can do this in a stand mixer or using a hand-held electric whisk. You can also do this by hand, but it does take time and lots of elbow grease! You want the mixture to be light and fluffy and to turn pale in colour.

Once the butter and the sugar are creamed, add the crème fraiche and stir together to just combine. Add about half of the flour along with the baking powder and three eggs and beat everything together until it is just combined. Then add the other three eggs and flour and mix, again until just combined.

Using a spatula, divide the cake mixture between the lined tins and bake in the oven for 25–30 minutes, or until a skewer inserted into the centre of each cake comes out clean, and the sponges have shrunk slightly from the edges of the tin.

About 10 minutes before the cakes are cooked, make the syrup. Put the caster sugar, water and rum into a small pan over a low heat. Cook gently until the sugar has dissolved, then turn up the heat and let it bubble for 20 seconds or so, then take it off the heat.

The trick is not to over-work the mixture, otherwise the gluten in the flour starts to get tough and your cake will not be super light and fluffy – although it will still taste good!

>

RUM & COCONUT CAKE WITH TOASTED COCONUT FLAKES

Once the cakes are cooked, remove them from the oven and brush with the rum syrup. This will make the cakes more moist and also gives them extra flavour. The added bonus is that the cakes will keep for a little longer too. Once you have brushed the cakes with the rum syrup, then leave them to cool completely in the tins.

While the cakes are cooling in the tins, make the buttercream frosting. Put the butter into a bowl and add a little of the icing sugar and beat well to combine. Keep doing this, adding a little bit of icing sugar as you go so that the icing sugar does not fly everywhere. Alternatively you can put all the buttercream ingredients into the bowl of a stand mixer fitted with a paddle attachment and then cover the machine with a tea towel and beat it like mad, keeping the tea towel over the machine, but being careful not to let the towel get stuck in any moving parts. I like a very light buttercream frosting for this cake, so I always beat it for quite some time until it is extremely light and fluffy, which also makes it much easier to spread.

Smear a little of the frosting on your cake stand or plate – just a splodge to secure the first sponge. Put one of the cake layers on top, and using a palette knife, spread some more of the buttercream frosting all over the top. Repeat this twice more so you have a three-layer cake. Be careful not to press the layers down much as you are building the cake as this can make the cake bulge in places.

Spread the rest of the buttercream frosting all over the sides. It does not have to be super smooth as you are going to put the toasted coconut flakes on it. You can make the buttercream as thick or as thin as you fancy, but if you are doing it on the thin side, just remember that you need enough buttercream to stick the flakes on.

Take a handful of the toasted coconut flakes and press them onto the side of the cake – some will fall down but that is okay. Keep pressing the flakes all over the sides of the cake and all over the top of the cake until the whole of the cake is covered. Serve.

Don't confuse beautiful coconut flakes with desiccated coconut. Some supermarkets do not sell large coconut flakes, but I have found them in most high-street health-food shops and online.

NAKED RED VELVET LAYER CAKE & CREAM CHEESE FROSTING KISSES

SERVES 12–20

What, more red velvet? Yes, more red velvet – I would make all of my baking red if I could. Red food literally makes me so happy. I have experimented with many food colourings and Sugarflair is the only one I have found that makes things super red. Cream cheese frosting can be tricky to make as it goes soft very quickly, so if you find this happening to you, pop it in the fridge for a few moments to firm up.

Preheat the oven to 180°C (fan 160°C/350°F/gas 4). Line the base of the three cake tins with baking parchment. Cream together the butter and caster sugar until light and fluffy. You can do this for 5 minutes in a stand mixer or using a hand-held electric whisk. You can also do this by hand, but it takes about 10 minutes and lots of elbow grease! Add five of the eggs and half of the flour to the creamed butter and sugar and beat well together. Then add the remaining eggs and the rest of the flour and beat well again until well combined.

Add enough red food colouring to the mixture, stirring all the time, until the sponge is a lovely red colour. The red will turn a little darker in the oven but it will not get any more 'red'. So if the mixture still looks pink then just add more colouring. I usually use about 1 teaspoon of colouring, which is quite a lot, but necessary if you want to get the right colour.

Divide the mixture evenly between the lined cake tins and smooth the tops with the back of a spoon. Place in the oven and bake for 25–30 minutes or until a skewer inserted into the centre of each cake comes out clean.

Place baking parchment on two wire racks. When the cakes are baked remove them from the oven. Leave them to cool for a few moments and then remove them from the cake tins. Place each cake, bottom side up, onto the baking parchment on the wire rack. This will help the cakes stay nice and flat. You may find that the sides of the cakes have gone a bit brown, if so, I like to take a very fine microplane grater and gently rub the sides of the cake to 'shave off' the brown colour and expose the brilliant red underneath.

If you find that your cakes are not flat, then just use the microplane grater to carefully grate off any 'humps' – the cut-off cake bits can be a baker's perk!

>

450g butter, softened

450g caster sugar

9 eggs

450g self-raising flour

½–1 tsp red food colouring (I always use Sugarflair red extra or Christmas red)

For the cream cheese frosting

220g butter, softened

500g icing sugar

220g soft cream cheese (I use Philadelphia)

Equipment

3 x 20cm round loose-bottomed cake tins

hand-held electric whisk or stand mixer

fine microplane grater (optional)

piping bag with a 1cm plain nozzle

NAKED RED VELVET LAYER CAKE & CREAM CHEESE FROSTING KISSES

While the cakes are cooling, make the frosting. Use a hand-held electric whisk or put the butter into a stand mixer and beat well until very soft and light. Add the icing sugar in four batches, beating well between each addition. I like to cover the mixer with a damp tea towel so that the icing sugar does not fly everywhere!

Once the butter and the icing sugar are well combined add the cream cheese and beat until just combined. The frosting will most probably be super soft at this stage so put it in the fridge to firm up a little so that it is nice and easy to pipe.

Once the cakes have cooled, half-fill the piping bag with the frosting – filling halfway ensures that the frosting does not squidge out of the top when you are piping.

Remove the baking parchment from the cake layers and pipe large kisses on top of each cake. Stack the layers on top of each other, being careful not to press down, to keep the kisses intact. If the frosting is too soft it will squish down when you layer the cakes and you won't be able to see the beautiful individual kisses, so if this happens, pop the cakes and frosting in the fridge for 10–15 minutes or so to firm up. Once the cakes are stacked together, put a blob of frosting onto your serving plate or cake stand, then carefully transfer the whole cake onto it, and serve.

To pipe kisses, hold the nozzle about 5mm from the surface of the cake and then squeeze the piping bag. When the kiss is the right size, stop squeezing the piping bag and lift off the nozzle.

DEATH BY CHOCOLATE FUDGE CAKE WITH CHOCOLATE GANACHE DRIZZLE

There are chocolate cakes that are light, moist and fluffy, with an echo of chocolate on the aftertaste … and there are others like this one that are deep in flavour, moist and fudge-like, that you sink your teeth into and that just make you go 'yesssss!' Rich and unforgiving in its chocolatey-ness, one slice from this cake could never possibly be enough.

200g butter, softened

350g soft light brown sugar

seeds of ½ vanilla pod or ½ tsp vanilla extract

1 tsp Camp coffee essence (optional)

6 eggs (at room temperature)

280g wholemeal or regular self-raising flour

1 tsp baking powder

60g cocoa powder

210g crème fraiche (at room temperature)

For the chocolate frosting

120g dark chocolate, melted

180g butter, softened

375g icing sugar

2 tbsp double cream

For the chocolate ganache drizzle

140ml double cream

140g dark chocolate, roughly chopped, plus extra for grating

Preheat the oven to 180°C (fan 160°C/350°F/gas 4) and line the tins with baking parchment.

Put all of the ingredients for the sponge into a bowl and whisk well until combined. You can do this in a stand mixer or using a hand-held electric whisk. You can also do this by hand, but it does take time and lots of elbow grease! Using a spatula, divide the mixture between the lined tins, smoothing down the tops.

Bake for 25–30 minutes, until the cakes are springy to the touch and a skewer inserted into the centre of each cake comes out clean. Cool for 5 minutes in the tins, then turn out onto a wire rack and leave to cool completely.

When the cakes have cooled, mix together the chocolate frosting ingredients. I use my stand mixer with a paddle attachment and beat it for a good 5 minutes, until light and spreadable. You can do this by hand but it will take longer.

Smear a little of the frosting on your cake stand or plate – just a splodge to secure the first sponge. Place a cake layer on top and spread it with a little more frosting. Cover with another cake layer and more frosting.

Top with the remaining cake layer, flipping it over so that the flat side of the cake is now at the top. Very lightly press all the cake layers together, then use a palette knife to spread the remaining frosting evenly over the top and sides of the cake so that the sides are nice and straight and the top is flat. I like to do a thin layer first for a crumb-coating, and then place the cake in the freezer for 10 minutes for this layer to firm up.

> I like to flip the top cake over, so that you end up with a good flat base for frosting the top and sides.

>

DEATH BY CHOCOLATE FUDGE CAKE WITH CHOCOLATE GANACHE DRIZZLE

Equipment

3 x 20cm round cake tins

stand mixer or hand-held electric whisk (optional)

Take the cake from the freezer and add another thicker layer of the chocolate frosting, having a good play around with the knife so that it is really smooth. Sometimes it helps to run the palette knife under warm water and then carry on smoothing the frosting. Leave it to set a little while you make the ganache drizzle.

Heat the cream in a pan until it is just steaming, but don't boil it. Take the pan off the heat and add the chocolate, leaving it to melt for a few minutes, then stir the chocolate gently and let it cool down a little.

Pour the chocolate ganache drizzle over the cake so that it forms a smooth layer all over the top and then drips nicely down the sides of the cake. Grate over the chocolate and serve.

For a clean finish, don't press down too much on the cakes as you're frosting, as this can cause frosting to bulge out between each cake layer.

PECAN PIE POPCORN NAKED CAKE

I'm a judge for a show on the Food Network in the States called the 'Holiday Baking Championship', and I learn a lot from the contestants on the show. The following cake is called a naked cake, aptly named because it contains no cloak of buttercream to cover its naked crumb or umbrella of fondant to hide its nudity – it's delightfully rude, just like this combination of popcorn, pecan and rich creamy filling.

Preheat the oven to 180°C (fan 160°C/350°F/gas 4) and line the cake tins with baking parchment. Put the pecan nuts on a baking tray and roast in the oven for 8–10 minutes, checking them regularly and giving the tray a good shake halfway through cooking to ensure they cook evenly. Remove them from the oven and leave to cool, then chop roughly and set aside.

To make the sponge, cream together the butter and light brown sugar for 5 minutes, until light and fluffy. You can do this in a stand mixer or using a hand-held electric whisk. You can also do this by hand, but it does take time and lots of elbow grease! When the mixture is light and fluffy, add three of the eggs and half of the milk or water, the vanilla and half of the flour and beat together until just combined. Add the remaining four eggs, milk or water and flour, as well as the baking powder and stir, using as few stirs as possible so that the cakes remain light and fluffy. Using a spatula, fold in the toasted pecan nuts.

Divide the mixture between the lined tins and bake for 30–35 minutes, or until a skewer inserted into the centre of each cake comes out clean. Once the cakes are baked, remove them from the oven and leave them to cool down completely in the tins.

When the cakes have cooled, make the filling. Mix together the butter and cream cheese in a large bowl along with the icing sugar. Be careful not to over-stir, as the cream cheese thins if it is overworked. If the buttercream does get a little runny, then just place it into the fridge to firm up a bit.

Put a blob of the buttercream on a cake stand or serving plate and put the first cake layer on top of it. This will stop the cakes from moving around too much when you are layering. Spread a third of the buttercream over the top of the first cake and repeat with the other cakes, finishing with a layer of the buttercream on the top. Then pile the toffee popcorn on top and serve.

250g pecan nuts

350g butter, softened

325g soft light brown sugar

7 eggs

4 tbsp whole milk or water

seeds of 1 vanilla pod or 2 tsp vanilla extract

325g self-raising flour

½ tsp baking powder

100g toffee popcorn (Butterkist)

For the buttercream filling

75g butter, softened

250g full-fat cream cheese (I use Philadelphia)

125g icing sugar (sifted if lumpy)

Equipment

3 x 20cm round loose-bottomed cake tins

stand mixer or hand-held electric whisk (optional)

SACHERTORTE

People rarely make Sachertorte (Austrian mirror glaze cake) at home. It is more likely to be seen in the window displays of beautiful patisseries around the world. The method differs from the usual one for making a cake, as you mix the egg whites in separately to retain a super-light sponge. It is easy to do, but it takes a bit of juggling. The best bit, of course, is the chocolate glaze, dripping quickly down the sides of this very special cake.

Preheat the oven to 170°C (fan 150°C/325°F/gas 3) and line the base of the tins with baking parchment and spray the sides with a little oil. Put the chocolate in a large heatproof bowl set over a pan of simmering water to melt. Make sure the base of the bowl does not touch the simmering water, otherwise the chocolate may 'seize' into a big thick lump. When the chocolate has melted, remove the pan from the heat and allow to cool down to body temperature.

Once the chocolate has cooled, cream together the butter and icing sugar in a bowl until light and a little fluffy and set aside. Remove the bowl with the melted chocolate from the pan and then add the egg yolks to it and stir together with a spatula to just combine. Take the butter and sugar mixture and add this to the chocolate and egg mix and beat to combine. It might look as if it is not going to mix in at first but keep going and it will.

Once it is all mixed in, add the flour, folding it in gently with as few stirs as possible. The trick is not to over-work the mixture otherwise the gluten in the flour starts to get tough and your cake will not be super light and fluffy, although it will still taste good.

In a separate bowl add the egg whites, and using a hand-held electric whisk or a stand mixer fitted with a whisk attachment, whisk a little until frothy. Then add one quarter of the caster sugar at a time, whisking well between each addition, making sure that all of the sugar is dissolved before you add the next lot. Once all of the sugar has been added, keep whisking it until the mixture becomes firm and shiny. Some people say to hold the bowl over your head – if it doesn't fall out, it's ready!

Tip the meringue into the chocolate mixture and gently fold everything together, making sure it is all combined. Divide the mixture between the lined tins.

oil, for spraying

190g dark chocolate (at least 70% cocoa solids), finely chopped

150g butter, softened

80g icing sugar

8 egg yolks

150g plain flour

8 egg whites

85g caster sugar

4 tbsp apricot jam

For the chocolate glaze
180ml double cream

75g dark chocolate, finely chopped

75g milk chocolate, finely chopped

75g granulated sugar

125g butter, diced and at room temperature

30g glucose syrup or golden syrup

Equipment
2 x 20cm round cake tins

hand-held electric whisk or stand mixer

>

SACHERTORTE

Bake the cakes in the oven for 18–20 minutes, or until the cakes are springy to the touch, have shrunk slightly from the sides of the tin and a skewer inserted into the centre of each cake comes out clean. Once the cakes are baked, remove them from the oven.

Place a cooling rack upside down on top of both of the cakes. Holding onto both of the cakes and the cooling rack, flip everything over so that the cakes are now upside down on the cooling rack. Carefully remove the tins and then leave them to cool down like this completely – it will mean that the cakes are nice and flat.

When the sponges are cool, prepare the filling by gently heating the apricot jam in a small pan or in the microwave so that it is spreadable. Spread a sponge with warmed apricot jam, and then sandwich the other one on top. Place the cooling rack into a deep baking tray (to catch the excess chocolate glaze) and set aside.

To make the chocolate glaze, heat the cream in a pan over a medium heat until almost boiling. Then take it off the heat and add the dark and milk chocolate along with the sugar. Let it sit for a few moments and then using as few stirs as possible, stir it through to check that everything is melted.

When the chocolate has melted, add the butter a little at a time, stirring well between each addition until the glaze has thickened and is nice and shiny. This whole stage needs to be done quite quickly as the chocolate is ready when it reaches just body temperature. To test this temperature put a little on your lower lip and it should feel really warm but not hot to the touch.

I pour it over the middle of the cake to start with and find that the more you pour it, the force pushes the chocolate glaze over the edges of the cake and down the sides. You may have to pour the chocolate around the edges at the end to make sure all bits are covered.

Leave the Sachertorte to set at room temperature because if you put it in the fridge it can dull the beautiful mirror-like glaze, and then serve.

There will be lots of glaze in the bottom of the baking tray, but this is fine and can be scooped up and reheated to serve on ice cream if you fancy it!

VANILLA & WHITE CHOCOLATE NAKED CAKE WITH BLUEBERRY BUTTERCREAM

This is a truly beautiful cake, perfect for a real celebration, such as a wedding or engagement. The trick is to create neat blueberry buttercream layers, and to choose flowers that complement the purply blue of the frosting. Make sure that your choice of flowers is safe to use on a cake.

450g butter, softened

450g caster sugar

7 eggs

seeds of 2 vanilla pods or 4 tsp vanilla extract

I tsp baking powder

2 tbsp Greek yoghurt

2 tbsp milk

300g self-raising flour

pinch of salt

150g white chocolate, melted

fresh flowers, to decorate

For the vanilla syrup

75g granulated sugar

75ml water

seeds of I vanilla pod or 2 tsp vanilla extract

For the blueberry buttercream

200g blueberries

2 tbsp caster sugar

50ml water

300g butter, softened

600g icing sugar

Preheat the oven to 180°C (160°C fan/350°F/gas 4) and line the base of the cake tins with baking parchment. Cream together the butter and caster sugar until light and fluffy. You can do this for 5 minutes in a stand mixer or using a hand-held electric whisk. You can also do this by hand, but it takes about 10 minutes and lots of elbow grease!

Add two of the eggs with the vanilla, baking powder, and half of the yoghurt, milk and flour. Beat well together, and then add the remaining eggs with the rest of the yoghurt, milk and flour and beat well again until evenly combined. Add a pinch of salt, beat for a moment and then fold in the melted chocolate. Divide the mixture evenly between the lined cake tins and smooth the tops with the back of a spoon. Bake the cakes in the oven (in batches if necessary) for 25–35 minutes, or until golden and a skewer inserted into the centre of each cake comes out clean.

As the cakes are baking, make the vanilla syrup. Put the granulated sugar into a small pan with the water and vanilla over a low heat. Heat gently until the sugar has dissolved, stirring, and then turn up the heat and bring to the boil. Allow this to bubble away for 2 minutes and then take it off the heat and set aside to cool a little.

When the cakes are baked, remove them from the oven and brush them liberally with the vanilla syrup to give the cake a beautifully moist crumb. Set the cakes aside to cool down completely.

As the cakes are cooling, prepare the blueberry puree for the buttercream. Put the blueberries, caster sugar and water into a small pan and cook over a low heat for 5 minutes, until the blueberries have broken down and become mushy, stirring occasionally. Increase the heat and boil the blueberry mixture for another 5 minutes, stirring occasionally, then remove from the heat and leave it to cool down a little.

>

VANILLA & WHITE CHOCOLATE NAKED CAKE WITH BLUEBERRY BUTTERCREAM

Equipment

3 x 20cm round loose-bottomed cake tins

hand-held electric whisk or stand mixer (optional)

blender

cake scraper (optional)

Blitz the cooled mixture in a blender to a smooth puree and pass it through a fine sieve into a bowl. Set aside until needed. You should end up with about 5–6 tablespoons of puree.

To finish the buttercream, place the butter and icing sugar in a bowl (or I like to use a stand mixer) and then beat it like mad until the mixture becomes pale and fluffy. Gently fold all of the blueberry puree into the buttercream until evenly combined. The buttercream needs to be nice and thick to achieve dramatic thick layers between the cakes.

When the cakes are completely cool, remove one from the tin and put it on a serving plate or cake stand, sticking it down with a little buttercream so the cake does not move around. Spread over one-third of the blueberry buttercream in a thick even layer and place another cake on top.

Spread another third of the blueberry buttercream in another thick layer on top and finish with the final cake. Top with a final layer of buttercream, and use a cake scraper or palette knife to smooth the sandwiched blueberry buttercream over the side of the cake to give a very thin coating. The cake should be naked, so you don't want loads of buttercream on the sides but aim to end up with a very, very thin see-through layer.

When you are happy with the cake and the outside looks smooth, decorate the top of the cake with a nice arrangement of fresh flowers and serve.

BASICS

BRITISH VANILLA BUTTERCREAM

This is the simplest of all the buttercream recipes. With just a couple of ingredients and a good beating, everyone is a winner. Well-made buttercream has always been my favourite part – the rich, sweet naughty creaminess is hard to beat. When I had my bakery we would always use the same quantities for the vanilla buttercream: half butter to sugar, plus flavourings. This makes enough buttercream to cover a three-layer 20cm cake.

Place the butter and vanilla together in a large bowl or stand mixer. If you are using a hand-held electric whisk, then add the icing sugar little by little as you whisk so that the icing sugar does not fly everywhere, and whisk well between additions.

If you are using a stand mixer, fit it with a paddle attachment, then add the icing sugar in one go and carefully place a tea towel over the machine, taking care not to get it anywhere near the paddle. Start mixing slowly at first, and then beat it for a good 5–7 minutes. Remove the tea towel when the icing sugar is all mixed in.

When the buttercream is super light and fluffy, use as desired. It keeps at room temperature for 3 days, or up to 2 weeks in the fridge covered with cling film. It freezes really well – defrost it at room temperature or overnight in the fridge (not in the microwave), then beat it again until light and fluffy before using.

300g butter, softened

seeds of ½ vanilla pod or l tsp vanilla extract

600g icing sugar

Equipment
hand-held electric whisk or stand mixer

I like to whisk my buttercream until it is super light and airy. This not only makes it taste better, but it also makes more buttercream, so you can use it to ice more cakes and cupcakes!

CLASSIC AMERICAN BUTTERCREAM

This recipe can be found on cakes and cupcakes all over the States. It is super rich due to the addition of what Americans refer to as 'heavy' cream (double cream), but, if you prefer, you can substitute the cream with milk. For different flavour options, feel free to add ingredients such as almond extract, Camp coffee essence or the zest of one lemon or orange. As a guide, this makes enough buttercream to cover a two-layer 20cm cake.

Place the butter, vanilla and double cream or milk together in a large bowl or stand mixer. If you are using a hand-held electric whisk, then add the icing sugar little by little as you whisk so that the icing sugar does not fly everywhere, whisking well between additions.

If you are using a stand mixer, fit it with a paddle attachment, then add the icing sugar in one go and carefully place a tea towel over the machine taking care not to get it anywhere near the paddle. Beat it hard until it is light and well combined, scraping down the sides of the bowl with a spatula to ensure it is evenly combined. Remove the tea towel when the sugar is all mixed in.

When the buttercream is super light and fluffy, use as desired. It keeps at room temperature for 3 days, or up to 2 weeks in the fridge covered with cling film.

200g unsalted butter, softened

seeds of ½ vanilla pod or 1 tsp vanilla extract

3 tbsp double cream or whole milk

475g icing sugar

Equipment

hand-held electric whisk or stand mixer

AMERICAN 'CRUSTING' BUTTERCREAM FROSTING

This is a fabulous base for covering big cakes. It may seem odd at first to add shortening to icing, however, for perfectly frosted, big American-style cakes, this variety is the only answer for me. The butter adds flavour, but if you prefer an ultra white buttercream, you can replace the butter with more vegetable shortening. This recipe makes enough buttercream to cover a three-layer 30cm cake – enough to fill between the layers and cover.

110g butter, softened

350g vegetable shortening, softened (such as Trex, Flora White or Cookeen)

seeds of 1–1½ vanilla pods or 2–3 tsp vanilla extract

900g icing sugar

80ml whole milk, plus a little extra if desired

Equipment

stand mixer or hand-held electric whisk

Put the butter, vegetable shortening and vanilla into the bowl of the stand mixer fitted with a paddle attachment. Turn the machine on to a medium speed and mix together for a good 5 minutes. Halfway through the mixing process, scrape down the sides of the bowl using a spatula. You can also mix this buttercream with a hand-held electric whisk, but you will need a very big bowl, and when it comes to adding the icing sugar it can get pretty messy.

Add one third of the icing sugar to the butter mixture. To stop the icing sugar from flying everywhere, cover the machine with a tea towel, taking care not to get it anywhere near the paddle attachment. This technique prevents icing sugar from going all over the kitchen, but you can remove the tea towel when the icing sugar is all mixed in. Add the icing sugar, little by little, until it is all mixed in. Start with a very slow speed and when the mixture starts to combine, increase the speed to high. Then add the milk and beat until well combined, scraping down the sides of the bowl with a spatula. If you prefer your buttercream to be thin, you can add more milk, tablespoon by tablespoon, mixing well between each addition until it reaches the consistency you require.

The buttercream is now ready to use and will keep at room temperature for 3 days, or up to 2 weeks in the fridge covered with cling film.

When you're ready to use the prepared buttercream, half-fill a piping bag to frost your cake. Once you have finished frosting the cake, it will take 30–45 minutes to form a relatively firm crust.

It's worth checking out online tutorials before deciding on the piping effect you would like, and trying a couple of practice runs on 'dummy' cakes before tackling the real thing.

CREAM CHEESE BUTTERCREAM

MAKES ABOUT 1KG

This is the 'one and only' for carrot cakes, and is often used on red velvet cupcakes. It has a slightly sour flavour that can offset the richness of the butter and the sweetness of the sugar. Its texture is looser than traditional British buttercream; the more you whip the cream cheese, the runnier it gets, so once you've added it, whip it just enough to combine and you are good to go. This makes enough frosting to generously cover a three-layer 20cm cake.

Place the butter and vanilla together in a large bowl or stand mixer. If you are using a hand-held electric whisk, then add the icing sugar little by little so that the icing sugar does not fly everywhere, and mix well between additions.

If you are using a stand mixer, fit it with a paddle attachment, then add the icing sugar in one go and carefully place a tea towel over the machine, taking care not to get it anywhere near the paddle. Beat well for 5–7 minutes, until the mixture is really light and fluffy.

When the buttercream is light and fluffy and the icing sugar is all mixed in, add the cream cheese and beat it for another minute or so.

Your cream cheese buttercream is now ready to use. The buttercream keeps at room temperature for 2 days, or up to 1 week in the fridge covered with cling film. Use as required. This buttercream usually gets used up quickly in my house, but if you need to you can freeze it and defrost it overnight in the fridge before use.

Maple syrup cream cheese buttercream

To make maple syrup cream cheese buttercream, simply add 5 tablespoons of maple syrup to the bowl with the butter.

250g butter, softened

seeds of ½ vanilla pod or 1 tsp vanilla extract

550g icing sugar

250g cream cheese (I use Philadelphia)

Equipment
hand-held electric whisk or stand mixer

ITALIAN MERINGUE VANILLA BUTTERCREAM

This is made from an Italian meringue, which produces a stable and very silky buttercream. It's perfect for show-stoppers such as wedding cakes and is one of my favourite buttercreams for piping, because it is very easy to work with. You can also make it well in advance. It takes a little bit of time, but the end result is worth it! As a guide, this makes enough buttercream to cover a two-layer 20cm cake.

220g granulated sugar

90ml water

4 egg whites, at room temperature

pinch of cream of tartar

220g butter, softened

seeds of 1 vanilla pod or 2 tsp vanilla extract

Equipment

sugar thermometer (optional)

stand mixer or hand-held electric whisk

Put the sugar and water in a small pan over a low heat and allow the sugar to dissolve. Once the sugar is dissolved, increase the heat and bring to the boil. Use a wet brush to brush the sugar from the sides of the pan.

Use a sugar thermometer to measure when the temperature reaches 120–122°C (250–252°F). If you do not have a sugar thermometer you can check that it is ready by placing ½ teaspoon of the syrup into a mug of cold water. Wait 15 seconds for it to harden and then use your fingers to pull out the sugar syrup – it should have formed a little ball that is firm to the touch. If the ball does not form, then the sugar syrup needs to be cooked for longer.

As the sugar syrup cooks, put the egg whites into the bowl of a stand mixer fitted with a whisk attachment and beat on low–medium speed until foamy. Add the cream of tartar and whisk on a medium–high speed until medium–stiff peaks form (but not until they are super stiff). As soon as the sugar syrup reaches the correct temperature, remove it from the heat, and then, with the mixer running, add one fifth of it into the beaten egg whites. Whisk the egg white mixture to form stiff peaks and then gradually continue to add the sugar syrup in a thin steady stream, making sure that the sugar syrup does not touch the whisk or the sides of the bowl. Use the full amount of the sugar syrup and make sure that it does not get lost around the sides of the pan. If you are using a hand-held electric whisk, add the sugar syrup one quarter at a time, making sure that the egg whites are whisked to stiff peaks between each addition.

Once all the sugar syrup has been added, continue to beat on high speed for about 5 minutes, until the meringue has cooled right down to room temperature. Add the butter 1 tablespoon at a time, beating until smooth after each addition. Keep going until you have added all of the butter and then add the vanilla, beating the buttercream for another good 2–3 minutes. It will keep at room temperature for 3 days, or up to 2 weeks in the fridge covered with cling film. Use as required.

POURING FONDANT ICING

You can make pouring fondant icing from fondant icing powder, which is available in supermarkets under the Silver Spoon range. However, it is also extremely easy to make your own and then flavour it with whatever you fancy – including chocolate, which always goes down well!

Sift the icing sugar into a large bowl. Make a well in the centre and add the egg white and the liquid glucose. Beat, drawing the icing sugar into the centre until the mixture creates quite a stiff paste.

Turn the paste out onto a board that is lightly dusted with sifted icing sugar, and knead until the paste loosens. Return the paste to a bowl and beat in enough of the water until you have achieved the right pouring consistency. Use as required.

450g icing sugar, plus extra for dusting

I egg white

50g liquid glucose (at room temperature)

4–5 tsp water

Chocolate fondant pouring icing

To make chocolate pouring fondant icing, mix equal parts pouring fondant icing with equal parts melted dark chocolate.

CREME CHANTILLY

This is the first French pastry cream I learnt how to make and quite possibly the simplest. The secret is to use the cream straight from the fridge and also not to over-whip the mixture. If you can, whisk the crème Chantilly in a chilled glass or stainless steel bowl, although the recipe will still work if you don't.

200ml double or whipping cream (avoid extra thick cream as it does not whisk successfully)

2 tbsp icing sugar

seeds of ½ vanilla pod or I tsp vanilla extract

Equipment
hand-held electric whisk or stand mixer (optional)

Put the cream into a bowl with the icing sugar and vanilla and whisk on a medium–high speed using either a hand-held electric whisk or a stand mixer fitted with a whisk attachment. At cookery school we did it by hand with an ordinary whisk and it works just as well. Nothing will seem like it is happening for a minute or so (if doing by machine) or a few minutes (if doing by hand) but then the mixture will start to thicken. At this stage, keep an eye on it and, if using a mixer or hand-held electric whisk, keep it on a slow setting because it can go from being quite watery to super thick and over-whipped in a few seconds!

The crème Chantilly should have medium peaks while still being shiny and soft. I always stop whisking a little before the mixture is ready, as it will thicken slightly as it sits. If you find you have over-whisked it, simply add I tablespoon or so more cream or milk to thin it out again. If it turns yellowish in colour then you have really gone past the point of no return and congratulations – you have made your own butter! It's not quite what we want from crème Chantilly, but it is good to know what is possible!

Use the crème Chantilly as required.

I like to serve crème Chantilly with desserts, inside brandy snaps (with the addition of some Armagnac), on cakes or with something simple such as a bowl of fruit.

SWISS MERINGUE

During my degree at catering school, we learned that there are two ways to make Swiss meringue. One way is to heat the mixture using a blowtorch and the oven, but I find that sugar crystallizes and becomes hard and lumpy. I much prefer the method below, using a bain-marie and sugar thermometer. As long as you use an accurate probe thermometer, it is foolproof. You can use this recipe on top of Key lime meringue pie (see page 99).

120g egg whites (about 4 egg whites)

240g caster sugar

Equipment
sugar thermometer
stand mixer (optional)

Fill a medium pan with 5cm of water and place it on the hob. Bring the water to the boil over a high heat, and as soon as it is boiling, reduce to a simmer. Meanwhile, put the egg whites and sugar in a heatproof bowl and whisk them up until they become light and frothy.

Put the bowl over the now simmering water and keep whisking all the time until the temperature reaches 70°C (160°F) on your sugar thermometer. This will take 5–7 minutes. Once it has reached this temperature, remove the meringue from the heat and keep whisking until the mixture has cooled down and has become very thick, glossy and almost marshmallow-like in texture. It will take about 10–15 minutes to do this stage by hand, or once the mixture has reached 50°C (121°F) you can pop it into the bowl of a stand mixer with a whisk attachment, and whisk at high speed until it is body temperature and stiff peaks have formed – this will take about 6–8 minutes.

To check that it is ready, take some of the meringue on the end of the whisk, then turn the whisk meringue-covered end up – the meringue should be super stiff and not floppy. Some say to hold the bowl over your head – if none comes out then it is ready!

Use the Swiss meringue as required.

TEMPERING CHOCOLATE

Have you ever bought a bar of chocolate only to find that the chocolate has a funny white colour on it? This means that the chocolate has 'bloomed', which is what happens when it melts and then hardens at incorrect temperatures. There are various ways to temper chocolate so that it is shiny and has that 'snap' – here is the easy method known as 'seeding' that you can do without a thermometer, followed by a more accurate method.

Seeding method

This is not the most accurate way to temper chocolate, but it is easy and a very good place to start.

Melt two-thirds of the chocolate in a bain-marie. To make the bain-marie, fill a pan one third full with water and place it over a low heat. Then place a glass or metallic bowl on top, making sure that the bottom of the bowl does not touch the water. Once the water is barely simmering, add the chocolate and leave it to sit until the chocolate has completely melted.

Once the chocolate has melted, remove the bowl from the bain-marie but keep the heat on low. Place the bowl on the work surface and add the remaining one third of the chocolate to it. Stir gently until all of the chocolate has melted. Keep stirring it, and then check that it is ready by dabbing some on your inner wrist – it should feel very warm. Use the tempered chocolate as you need to, keeping in mind that the chocolate must remain at this temperature to be 'in temper'.

If the chocolate starts to firm up around the sides of the bowl and becomes thick and hard to stir, then you know that it has come out of temper, so pop it back on the bain-marie for a moment or so now and again, not allowing it to go any higher or lower than the 'warm wrist' temperature.

If it becomes too cool, then you will need to temper the chocolate all over again. To do this, melt the chocolate in your bowl again. Following the same ratio of two-thirds melted to one third solid chocolate, add another third of solid chocolate to the melted chocolate and repeat the tempering process again until it reaches the correct temperature.

300g dark chocolate (not cooking chocolate and at least 64% cocoa solids), or good-quality white chocolate, roughly chopped

Equipment
sugar thermometer (optional)

Thermometer method

This method is more accurate, but you do need a sugar thermometer. Melt all of the chocolate in a bain-marie (see opposite), stirring until you reach a temperature of 46–49°C (92–98°F). Then set the bowl with the melted chocolate into an ice bath (a larger bowl filled with some ice and water) and bring the temperature down to 27°C (80°F). Finally, put the bowl back on the heat and allow the melted chocolate to come back up to 31°C (88°F). The chocolate is now tempered and ready to use.

When you are tempering white chocolate with a thermometer, temperatures differ slightly. First of all you need to melt white chocolate in a bain-marie until it reaches 40-45°C (105–113°F), then you will need to bring the temperature down to 26–27°C (79–81°F) in the ice bath. Finally, bring the temperature of the chocolate back up to 29–30°C (84–86°F) over the bain-marie. The white chocolate is now tempered and ready to use.

CHOCOLATE DECORATIONS

You can make these delights up to 24 hours in advance and layer them up in baking parchment in a large airtight container. Make sure that none of the decorations touch each other or they may be damaged. Keep the container in a cool place, but not in the fridge or the chocolate may lose some of its sheen.

Dark chocolate curls

Spread the tempered chocolate into a thin, even layer on a sheet of acetate paper. When the chocolate is just beginning to set, cut it into 5mm strips with the trellis wheel or a very sharp knife. Carefully roll up the acetate of chocolate and secure it with tape until the chocolate is set. Once the chocolate is set, carefully open out the acetate paper and the chocolate curls will drop out. Use as required.

Striped chocolate cigarettes

Pour a thin line of tempered white chocolate down the centre of the work surface. I like to use a small marble slab because it cools the chocolate quickly and evenly, but you can use a marble or quartz work surface or the back of a flat baking sheet. Use the spatula or a palette knife to spread the chocolate into quite a thin layer. Spread it out, stretching from left to right rather than from top to bottom. Then use the cake-decorating comb to run through it from left to right, make sure you press right down to the bench leaving you with just stripes of white chocolate. Then let it firm up for a moment or two.

When the white chocolate has firmed up (it needs to be quite firm otherwise when you add the dark chocolate it will become marbled rather than giving you definitive lines) add the tempered dark chocolate on top and then using the angled palette knife work the dark chocolate into the lines of white chocolate, filling in all the gaps in a nice even thickness and using the palette knife to scrape off any excess. Take a sharp knife and clean up the edges of the large rectangle shape so it is neat for when you make the cigarettes.

300g tempered white and/or dark chocolate (see pages 266–7)

Equipment for the curls
acetate paper
trellis wheel (optional)

Equipment for the chocolate cigarettes
marble slab (optional)
large flexible spatula (optional)
cake-decorating comb
angled palette knife
metal bench scraper

Equipment for the piped chocolate decorations
acetate (optional)
disposable piping bag

Equipment for the chocolate leaves
fine paintbrush
tweezers

Wait until the chocolate is no longer soft and then take the bench scraper in both hands. Position the blade 2.5cm or so from the far end of the chocolate. Hold the blade at about a 25° angle from the surface. Working quickly and firmly, and with consistent pressure, push the bench scraper away from you, causing the chocolate to roll over itself. Keep forming cigarettes, working quickly so that the chocolate doesn't get too hard. Repeat this process until you have as many cigarettes as you need. The good news is that although these may sound like they are difficult to make, they take very little time and will get easier with practice!

Piped chocolate decorations

Line a large baking sheet with acetate or baking parchment. Fill the disposable piping bag with tempered dark chocolate and snip off the end. Then use this to pipe patterns and designs with the chocolate, making them 2.5–5cm in size. Keep practising to create consistent designs. Leave to set and use as required.

Chocolate leaves

Using the paintbrush, paint bay or sturdy mint leaves with tempered dark chocolate (or you could paint half with tempered white chocolate and the other half with tempered dark chocolate). Prop the painted leaves against an object, such as the handle of a wooden spoon, to create slightly curved leaves. Leave to set and then use tweezers to carefully peel the chocolate leaf from the bay or mint leaf, discarding the leaves. Use as required.

RICH SHORTCRUST PASTRY

MAKES ABOUT 400G

This is a quick and simple recipe for a light and tasty pastry. It is great for savoury flans and tarts and literally takes just minutes to make. If you prefer, replace the plain flour with spelt flour, which is easier to digest. One of the oldest cultivated grains in the world, spelt is becoming more widely available. It has a naturally higher composition of vitamins, and requires a special processing method, so is more expensive than regular flour.

The best way to make this pastry is in a food processor. Pop the flour, salt and butter into the food processor and pulse it in quick bursts until the mixture starts to resemble fine breadcrumbs. Add the egg yolks and 1 tablespoon of the water and pulse again until the mixture starts to come together. Add a little more water if the dough is still dry, but not too much otherwise your pastry will be tough.

If you are making this by hand, then put the flour, salt and butter into a bowl and rub the mixture together with your thumbs and fingers, letting the mixture fall back into the bowl. Keep doing this until the mixture resembles breadcrumbs, then add the egg yolks with 1 tablespoon of the water and use a round-bladed knife to mix it all together. Add a little more water if the dough is still dry, but not too much otherwise your pastry will be tough.

Tip the dough onto the work surface and bring it together into a ball. Wrap the ball in cling film and then gently press it down to flatten. Pop it into the fridge for 30 minutes for the mixture of stretchy proteins (gluten) in the dough to relax – this makes it much easier to roll out and also reduces the shrinkage in the oven. The pastry is now ready to use but you can keep the pastry wrapped in cling film in the fridge for up to a week. Use as required.

Sweet rich chocolate pastry

To make sweet chocolate shortcrust pastry, reduce the amount of flour to 200g, and the amount of butter to 120g. Follow the method above, but add 2 tablespoons of sifted cocoa powder and 2 tablespoons sifted icing sugar to the bowl with the other ingredients.

240g plain flour

pinch of fine salt

140g butter, cold and cut into cubes

2 egg yolks

1–2 tbsp ice-cold water

Equipment
food processor
(optional)

PUFF PASTRY

MAKES ABOUT 630G

In a number of my TV shows I have been seen to trundle off to the shops and buy shop-bought pastry to use as a base for my desserts and pastries. I honestly still think that's fine, but I also think it is important to have a go at making your own puff pastry – even if you only try it once. Sure, it does take a bit of time to do, but as they say … good things come to those who wait!

For the dough 'packet'

250g plain flour, plus extra for dusting

pinch of salt

35g butter, cold and cut into cubes

100–150ml ice-cold water

For the butter 'packet'

225g butter, at room temperature

To make the détrempe (dough packet), put the flour, salt and butter into a bowl and rub the mixture between your thumb and first two fingers, letting the mixture drop back in the bowl. Keep doing this until the mixture resembles breadcrumbs. Add 100ml of the water and mix it together with a round-bladed knife. If there are some dry bits of pastry in the bowl, then sprinkle with the remaining 50ml of water so that most of the pastry is no longer dry.

Bring the pastry together with your hands, until you reach a soft but not sticky or dry dough. Knead the dough for about 10 seconds and then form a basic dough ball – the détrempe. Using a sharp knife, cut a large cross in the top, which helps the mixture of stretchy proteins (gluten) in the flour to relax. Then wrap the détrempe in cling film and put it into the fridge for 1–1½ hours – this resting time makes the pastry easier to roll out later on.

To make the butter 'packet', gently soften the butter and then wrap it in cling film. Using the cling film to help you, shape it into a 9cm square. Put the square in the fridge for about 45 minutes to firm up a little. The butter packet needs to be pliable and at a similar consistency to the détrempe so that when you incorporate them they combine easily. If the butter is too hard it will make this difficult.

Once the détrempe has rested for 1–1½ hours, remove it from the fridge and roll it out to make a 20cm square on a lightly floured surface. Take the 9cm butter packet and put it in the centre of the détrempe square, at an angle so that a corner of the butter is facing the horizontal edge of the pastry – it should look like a kind of diamond from above. Placing it like this makes it easier to encase the butter.

Take each corner of the pastry to just past the centre so that all the corners overlap in the centre, encasing the butter. Put a little flour over the pastry

>

and then roll it out to form a rectangle about three times as long as it is wide (about 20 x 60cm). I like to use a palette knife to make sure that the edges are straight and the corners are at right angles. Roll the dough and push it into shape with the palette knife to get it just right.

With one of the short ends facing you, fold the bottom third of the pastry over the middle third and then fold the top third of the pastry down over the middle and bottom fold, giving you a package. Keep the dough moving and the surface lightly floured so that it does not stick to the surface, and use the palette knife to make sure the package has straight edges and right angles. Then turn the dough 90° to the right and roll it out again to another 20 x 60cm rectangle, using your palette knife to make it nice and straight. Repeat the folding again – bottom third up and top third down. Now the pastry has had two rolls and folds.

Wrap the pastry in cling film and pop it into the fridge again for the gluten to relax a little and for the butter to firm up a bit, although you want it to still be pliable. If the butter does poke through when you are doing your folds and gets too soft, then put the dough back into the fridge to firm up a little.

Do this process two more times, resting the pastry in between every two rolls and folds so that at the end of the process the pastry would have had a total of six rolls and folds. This process creates the layers that will puff up in the oven.

Once the pastry has been rested for a third time, it is ready to use. However, you can keep the pastry like this in the fridge wrapped in cling film for up to a week and it can be frozen for up to 6 weeks. Use as required.

CHOCOLATE PUFF PASTRY

You will need to set aside a bit of time to make this, but homemade chocolate puff pastry really is something else and it is a great recipe to have in your patisserie arsenal. For successful results, it is key that the dough packet (known as a 'détrempe') and chocolate butter packet reach a similar consistency.

For the dough 'packet'

25g butter

250g plain flour, plus extra for dusting

100ml water

1 tbsp white wine vinegar

pinch of salt

For the chocolate butter 'packet'

200g butter, slightly softened

50g cocoa powder (sifted if lumpy)

To make the détrempe (dough packet), melt the butter in a small pan or in the microwave and then set aside to cool. Put the flour into a large bowl and make a well in the centre. Add the water and mix it together with a wooden spoon. Then add the vinegar (this will help to give a more tender puff pastry) and the melted butter along with the salt and stir to combine.

Knead the dough for about 2–4 minutes and shape it into a 10 x 20cm rectangle. Wrap it in cling film and place it in the fridge for 1 hour to rest.

To make the chocolate butter 'packet', put the butter in a bowl and beat gently with a wooden spoon to cream it a little, then add the cocoa powder and beat everything together until it is evenly combined. Dollop this onto a piece of cling film and shape it into a 9cm square. Then wrap it up and pop it into the fridge for 30 minutes–1 hour to firm up a little.

Once the détrempe has rested for 1 hour, remove it from the fridge and roll it out to a 20cm square on a lightly floured surface. Then take the chocolate butter packet and put into the centre of the détrempe square, at an angle so that a corner of the butter is facing the horizontal side of the pastry – it should look like a kind of diamond from above.

Take each corner of the pastry to just past the centre so that all the corners overlap in the centre, encasing the butter. Press down on the puff pastry using a rolling pin to gently soften the butter a little, pressing as you go to lengthen the dough. Then roll the dough to form a rectangle about three times as long as it is wide (about 20 x 60cm).

With one of the short ends facing you, fold the bottom third of the pastry over the middle third and then fold the top third of the pastry down over the middle and bottom fold, giving you a package.

>

CHOCOLATE PUFF PASTRY

Use a palette knife to make sure the package has straight edges and right angles. Then turn the dough 90° to the right and roll it out again to another 20 x 60cm rectangle, using your palette knife to make it nice and straight. Repeat the folding again – bottom third up and top third down. Now the pastry has had two rolls and folds.

Wrap the pastry in cling film and pop it into the fridge again for the gluten to relax a little and for the butter to firm up a bit, although you want it to still be pliable. If the butter does poke through when you are doing your rolls and folds and gets too soft, then put the dough back into the fridge to firm up a little.

Do this process three more times, resting the pastry in between every two rolls and folds so that at the end of the process the pastry would have had a total of eight rolls and folds.

Once the pastry has rested for the fourth time it is ready to use. However you can keep the pastry like this in the fridge wrapped in cling film for up to a week and it can be frozen for up to 6 weeks. Use as required.

GLUTEN-FREE SHORTCRUST PASTRY

I only use one brand of gluten-free flour in the UK, and I am always pleased with the results. I think the trick when eating gluten-free pastry is not to compare it to regular pastry. Gluten-free pastry has its own personality, taste and texture. The recipe follows the standard formula for all shortcrust pastries: half fat to flour.

Put the flour, salt and butter into a food processor and pulse in quick bursts until the mixture starts to resemble fine breadcrumbs. Put the egg and water into a cup and beat to combine. Pour three-quarters of this egg mixture into the flour mixture and pulse again until the pastry comes together. If you feel the mixture needs a little more moisture, then add the rest of the liquid but if the pastry has already come together then there is no need. The dough should be nice and uniform in texture but not sticky.

Tip the dough onto a lightly floured surface and knead it gently for a few seconds to form a smooth dough, then wrap it in cling film, squish it down a little and pop it into the fridge for at least 1 hour. With gluten-containing flour, this stage is needed to relax the gluten in the pastry and therefore make it easier to roll out, but for this recipe we want the gluten-free flour to absorb the egg and the water to make it easier to use.

When the pastry has chilled, it is ready for use, or you can keep it wrapped in cling film in the fridge for up to a week.

It does not roll out like usual pastry – the best thing to do is to press it into the tin that you are using or, if you prefer, try rolling it out between two sheets of baking parchment. Once you have lined your tin, chill it for another 10 minutes before baking.

Use as required – I bake mine in an oven at 180°C (fan 160°C/350°F/gas 4) in the same way as regular pastry.

> For a sweet gluten-free shortcrust pastry, just stir in 1 tablespoon of caster sugar after you have pulsed the flour, salt and butter. You could also add the seeds of ½ a vanilla pod or 1 teaspoon of vanilla extract to the egg and water mixture, if desired.

220g gluten-free plain flour (I use Doves Farm)

pinch of salt

110g butter, cold and cut into cubes

1 egg, lightly beaten

2 tbsp ice-cold water, plus a little extra if necessary

Equipment
food processor

GLUTEN-FREE SWEET PASTRY WITH ALMONDS

Although this pastry is quite crumbly to work with, it has plenty of flavour. The trick is to blitz ground almonds into a fine texture, so that they become flour-like. For a gluten-free pastry without nuts, please see my Gluten-free shortcrust pastry (opposite).

180g ground almonds

2 tsp caster sugar

pinch of salt

70g butter, cold and cut into cubes

seeds of ½ vanilla pod or I tsp vanilla extract

I egg yolk

I tbsp ice-cold water (optional)

Equipment

food processor

Put the ground almonds into a food processor and pulse them until you have achieved a very fine texture, similar to almond flour. Then tip in the caster sugar, salt, butter and vanilla and pulse until the mixture starts to resemble fine breadcrumbs. Add the egg yolk and keep pulsing until the mixture just comes together. If the mixture still looks a bit dry after you've pulsed it a few times, then carefully scrape down the sides of the bowl and sprinkle the tablespoon of water over the dry parts, then pulse again.

Tip the mixture onto a work surface and squidge together into a ball. It is ready for use, or you can keep the pastry wrapped in cling film in the fridge for up to a week.

When rolling the pastry out, it helps to start by flattening it out with a wooden spoon, spatula or with your fingers.

Use as required – I bake mine in an oven that has been preheated to 180°C (fan 160°C/350°F/gas 4). If you are blind-baking this pastry (for instance if you want to add a filling and then bake it further), then bake it for about 10 minutes. However, if you want to bake the shell completely, bake it for 15–20 minutes until golden brown and then fill with custard, ganache or perhaps Crème Chantilly (see page 263).

LEMON CURD

Lots of my recipes call for lemon curd. Shop-bought is never as good as the one you make yourself. This is a wonderfully easy recipe that uses cornflour to thicken – this helps to keep it more stable and therefore much less likely to overcook. I really like using it in my recipes so I find that a batch is often worth making. I love spreading it onto toast in the morning for breakfast!

5 egg yolks

280g granulated sugar

zest and juice of 3 lemons

350ml boiling water

50g cornflour

1–2 tbsp cold water

Equipment

2 x 400g warm sterilized jars

Place the egg yolks and sugar in a bowl and whisk them together. You don't want lots of air in the mixture but just enough so that they are nicely combined. Whisk in the lemon zest and juice with the boiling water.

Put the cornflour into a mug and add enough of the cold water to mix it to a smooth paste – this process is called 'slaking' and ensures that the cornflour will mix in uniformly with the rest of the mixture.

Add the paste to the egg yolk mixture, stir everything together and then tip the mixture into a heavy-based pan. Slowly bring the mixture to the boil over a low–medium heat, whisking all the time, then simmer gently for 10 minutes, until the lemon curd is thick enough to coat the back of a wooden spoon, stirring constantly. Do not allow the mixture to boil, otherwise you may end up with lemony scrambled eggs!

Pour the curd into warm, sterilized jars and seal immediately. Store in the fridge for up to 3 weeks and use as required.

INDEX

Page numbers in **bold** denote an illustration.

I want to say a big thank you to all my family and friends.

Your love and continued support are everything.

Love you, Lorraine xxx

Follow me to
#bakeandshare
@lorrainepascale
@lorrainepascale
You Tube officiallpascale

First published 2017 by Bluebird
an imprint of Pan Macmillan
20 New Wharf Road, London N1 9RR
Associated companies throughout the world
www.panmacmillan.com

ISBN 978-1-5098-2073-3

9 8 7 6 5 4 3 2 1

A CIP catalogue record for this book is available from
the British Library.

Printed and bound in Italy.

Publisher Carole Tonkinson
Senior Editor Martha Burley
Senior Production Controller Ena Matagic
Art Direction & Design Jilly Topping
Prop Styling Lydia Brun
Food Styling Annie Rigg

Visit **www.panmacmillan.com** to read more about all our books
and to buy them. You will also find features, author interviews and
news of any author events, and you can sign up for e-newsletters
so that you're always first to hear about our new releases.